D✓NE

BEF✓RE

✓NE

DONE BEFORE ONE

HOW TO WORK SMARTER WHEN YOU WORK FOR YOURSELF

JASEN EDWARDS

Done Before One

Cover and interior design: Marko Markovic, www.5mediadesign.com

ISBN (paperback): 978-1-7364952-3-0
ISBN (ebook): 978-1-7364952-4-7
ISBN (audiobook): 978-1-7364952-5-4

Published by Jabari Life, LLC

www.JasenEdwards.com
www.DoneBeforeOne.com
Contact the author at hello@JasenEdwards.com.

Online resources for the major concepts presented
in this book can be downloaded at

www.DoneBeforeOne.com/bonus

CONTENTS

Introduction

YOUR NEW PRODUCTIVITY MANTRA: DONE BEFORE ONE

"When you arrive where you thought you wanted to be, you'll just begin a new journey. So enjoy each step along the way and keep in mind that every goal is possible from here. Just do one thing, one day at a time."

DR. WAYNE DYER

Have you ever arrived at the end of a day realizing you're exhausted but have gotten nothing important done? Have you ever fallen into a sales slump or found yourself in a general funk and wondered how you got there? Or how about this: Have you ever gone to work and felt guilty about what you're not handling at home, only to go home and feel guilty about what you didn't get done at work?

The bad news is that answering yes to any of those questions, or anything similar that came to mind as you read them, means there are fundamental flaws with how you're moving through your day. The good news is that you're normal. Everyone who works for themselves deals with productivity at work and integrating the rest of their lives, and the solution is simple. In fact, you're holding it!

The Done Before One (meaning before 1:00 p.m.) lifestyle is based on this basic premise: To be successful at work and have time for the rest of your life, you only need to control the first half of the day. Then let the afternoon fall apart if it must.

Here's why. Your mind operates like a smartphone battery; it runs best on a full charge. Therefore, to live the life you've always wanted, you must do your most important work before midday—before your body and mind attempt to go on power save mode or, in other words, experience the afternoon slump.

One of the biggest benefits of adopting a Done Before One lifestyle is that it brings your most important work into alignment with your natural energy pattern. When you pull your phone off the charger in the morning, it's working at full capacity until during the day it prompts you to go into power save mode where performance is intentionally limited to extend the time you have on your charge.

Likewise, when you wake up, your mind and body are at full charge. At some point during the middle of the day, you'll shift into power save mode yourself, also known as the afternoon slump. Once you've hit that slump, you won't be back to full charge until you've had a good night's sleep.

As addictive as smartphones can be, they aren't entirely to blame for your problems staying focused and productive. Anything you give your attention to is an input. Inputs draw down your mental energy just like tapping on a smartphone creates an input that runs code and draws down the battery. Most of us recharge our devices overnight, and sleeping overnight is how humans fully recharge.

The more people dive into bio-hacking and studying how to increase human lifespan and health span (extending good health throughout as many of your years as possible), the more we learn the importance of sleep. Experts attribute the afternoon slump and low energy that comes with it to events such as stress, a poor diet, a sedentary lifestyle, or more serious disorders like sleep apnea. Advice to overcome it ranges from taking a break from work to moving around, listening to upbeat music, drinking coffee, staying hydrated, intermittent fasting, taking ketones or other nootropics to boost brain function, or simply taking a nap.

All of this is sound advice and worthy of pursuing if you want to increase your energy and mood in the afternoon, but unfortunately we aren't like our cell phones in one important way. We can't just plug in for thirty to sixty minutes and get fully charged. If you plug in your phone midday, soon enough it'll recharge and work just as well as it did when you woke up.

When to Do Your Best Work

But all of those suggested ways to beat the afternoon slump, even power naps, just don't have the same effect for most people. You may get a boost, a significant one even, but you won't likely be in full power mode like you are when you first wake up. This means no matter how much caffeine you pump through your body, you will not be doing your best work later in the day. Because of this, the Done Before One lifestyle focuses on accomplishing your most important work for the day before the afternoon slump, when your brain goes into power save mode. From the moment you wake up, everything you give your attention to drains your mental and physical batteries. Even thoughts sitting in your unconscious mind—like worrying about money, friends, and family or events coming up in the near future—use up energy.

You must take responsibility for how you are using your charge. Do you want to use it while listening to the news? That's always so positive, isn't it? Would you say it's a good idea to use your freshly charged batteries by hopping on social media and comparing yourself to everyone else's highlight reel? But the responsible thing to do is to stay informed, right? So it's okay to check in with the news and witness humans tear each other down via the latest political fights and culture wars, isn't it? Ugh, no.

How about email? Going through your inbox is harmless, right? Right. Until you see that one message from a colleague that pisses you off or you realize you've just wasted thirty minutes scrolling through the last chance sale, which we all know is bullshit. Consumer goods always go on sale, but we still fall for the hype.

Obviously, none of these activities are helpful, and, more importantly, none of the tasks are based on your agenda. Even if you've somehow taught the social media algorithms to feed you only positive posts (and I'm not even convinced that's possible), you're still getting distracted by someone else's agenda.

With the Done Before One lifestyle, your agenda comes first, then the world's.

When you put your agenda first, you can access your creative mind and do your best work while your body and mind are fresh. Your best work brings you better (and usually faster) results. Then, when you respond to the outside world, your subconscious mind can take over and chew on the unresolved problems in the afternoon, evening, and overnight and bring you fresh inspiration the next morning.

Spend long enough in this pattern and you'll bump into more opportunities while ending each day feeling accomplished. The more days you end feeling proud of yourself for doing your best, the more your confidence and self-esteem will improve.

No doubt this is going to spill over into other areas of your life and have a positive impact on your experience in the world. The path to a fulfilling life can be pretty simple. And thank goodness for that, because none of us is getting any younger.

Live the Life Others Dream Of

You're about to learn how thousands of people before you have designed a lifestyle with harmony between their professional and personal worlds. There isn't any theory in this book. The method I describe was first created for my own individual use as a young self-employed salesman, then expanded to help my clients, all of whom are also self-employed. In fact, it's how I run my business and life to this day.

When and how you choose to tackle your most important work will determine if your professional life is fulfilling and funds the other parts of your life. So I want you to think of this book's title as your new productivity mantra. As you work through these pages and learn the method used by my clients and me, let it inspire and guide you into the lifestyle so many entrepreneurs and otherwise self-employed people dream of, but that few ever realize.

One more thing before we move on. When referring to the Done Before One lifestyle, I don't mean you should rush to finish every task on your projects list by literally 1:00 p.m. every single day. When you stop working each day is up to you, but if on the majority of days you can say you've accomplished your most important work by early afternoon, you'll be smashing through your goals. This book will show you exactly how to make that happen. But as you can imagine, *Done Before Sometime in the Early Afternoon* would have been a shitty (and forgettable) book title.

PART I

THE DONE BEFORE ONE LIFESTYLE

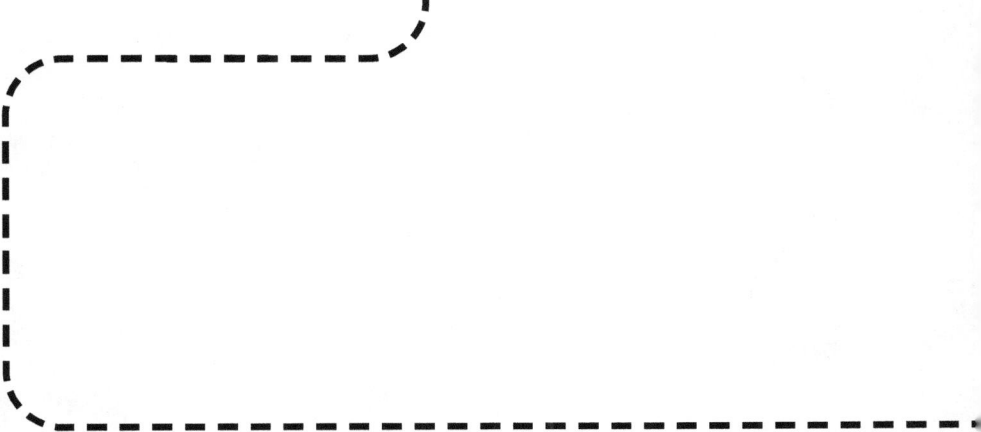

1

I WORK FOR MYSELF, NOW WHAT?

That's what this book is about—the principles and a method for your own powerful answer for how to work when you work for yourself. As long as you're able to confront your fears along the way, this will be the last book on productivity you'll need. But I almost didn't write it.

'll never forget the first day I walked into my office as a newly licensed real estate agent. I was eighteen years old, a literal teenager and self-employed. I was excited and convinced I'd soon be rich. I was also clueless about what to do. One of the many dirty secrets of the residential real estate industry is that once you get your license from the state, your real education starts.

If you're lucky, your broker will have an onboarding and training program that lasts a week or two. You'll learn about company policies, systems, and software, but it's rare to find a broker who has an effective sales training program. You'll have to learn to sell on your own. Rarer still is for anyone to teach you how to work. What I mean is, when you work for yourself, what in the world are you supposed to do every day?

In 1993, when I walked into my first office as a new real estate agent, I confronted that question for the first time. It was the very definition of a sink-or-swim environment, and no one was going to slow down long enough to give me an answer. Today I'm a long way from daily life as a real estate agent, and through my work as a performance coach, what I've learned for sure is that there are armies of people who answer the question of what to do each day incorrectly.

I've worked with a broad range of professionals, including real estate agents, loan officers, insurance salespeople, lawyers, retail sales reps, CEOs of large companies, government consultants, and entrepreneurs building amazing companies.

These folks were operating as either self-employed individuals or entrepreneurial leaders, and all of them at one time or another struggled with one similar challenge: how to do their work.

Growing up in America typically means we enter the workforce trained to follow instructions, complete checklists, and work in a linear fashion. The problem is our education prepared us for the Industrial Age and has left us ill-equipped to handle working in the modern world. We're taught to work all right, with skills for an era that's long gone.

People don't come to me for coaching when their personal and business lives are humming along as planned. Instead, they reach out when they're in trouble. Usually, that means they need more clients and customers. But sometimes it means they need their life back. They may have plenty of business but haven't taken a day off in three years. In both cases, the issue comes down to how they're spending their time daily.

You can obtain a PhD in your field, but if you do not learn to focus on the right tasks at the right time, all that education will be of no use to anyone. And if you muscle your way through the marketplace to build a business, you've likely done so at the expense of your personal life.

Everything is left to chance for people who don't have a good answer to the question "How do I do my work?". They're busy but not productive. They're easily influenced by other people's agendas. They end the day exhausted and start the next one tired and uninspired. They have a hard time holding appropriate boundaries and feel guilty when they try to take time off.

This leads to one of two places. Either you have a business that consumes your life to where you regret it, or you give up and take a job as a W-2 employee. Now listen, we need plenty of W-2 employees in the world. Everyone can't be the business owner. But if the idea of taking a regular paycheck makes you want to puke, you'll need a powerful answer to the question "How do I do my work?"

If that hits home for you, I have good news. Every self-employed person I've ever met has wrestled with this question. The great news is that you can learn how to be the successful badass you've always envisioned yourself to be while not sacrificing every other area of your life.

In fact, you can design your life so that your profession and your personal life enhance each other. Often when I begin working with someone, they feel their work and personal lives are in competition with each other. When seeking balance, what they're really looking for is an end to the stressful and self-created competition.

It's not helpful to think of your work and personal lives in terms of balance. Rarely are they ever balanced. They don't even need to be. And they certainly shouldn't be at war. But they can enhance each other so that you feel fulfilled in both. Here's a hint: there's more to it than finding the supposed perfect morning routine.

How Do I Know?

When I was a young man, long before I was concerned about my schedule or daily routines, I was a senior in high school who had all the credits I needed to graduate a semester early. That meant I technically didn't have to go to any classes during the final semester of my senior year. I don't remember exactly what I was saying to my parents at the time, but I do remember how, upon learning this, they worked quickly with the school to make sure I had a full-time job. Rather than let me drive all around Austin getting into trouble until graduation rolled around, they made sure to control my time, just as the school system had my entire childhood.

I'm a rebellious person by nature, but I didn't rebel against this decision being made for me because I already discovered I enjoyed earning money. I began working the moment it was lawful for me to do so and, like most American youth at the time, started in fast-food. My very first job was at some local hamburger joint whose name I can't even remember. Then came Little Caesar's and Subway.

Unlike today's youth with access to Uber and parents who seem to chauffeur them around at will, my main purpose for earning money was to buy a car. For teenagers in those days, a car, more than anything else, symbolized freedom.

By the time I was a senior, I had a car, and the faculty worked with my parents to direct me to my first professional office environment at the Texas Association of Realtors in downtown Austin. It was sort of glamorous driving into the parking garage of this luxurious office building right next to the state capital. The men wore suits; the women wore skirts and heels, and I ditched jeans, T-shirts, and my Subway apron for khakis and polos. It felt like a big step up from putting cheese and mayonnaise on bread.

I didn't know it but this was the beginning of my professional life. What I thought was a temporary high school job was, in fact, a springboard into a life where I had no choice but to learn how to work efficiently and effectively.

When I turned eighteen, I had already discovered my preference for work over college, but my time was still predominantly controlled by my class and work schedules. I attend class in the morning and clocked in for office work in the afternoon. This made 5:00 p.m. the best part of the day. Going down the elevator to my car and driving off to do what I wanted with my evening triggered an exhilarating feeling of freedom, especially if that day was Friday, with the entire weekend ahead.

But something else was happening around this time. Those who were in control of my work schedule—that is, my boss and his staff—were continually suggesting I'd be good at sales and encouraged me to get my real estate license. I'd never thought of being a Realtor as a career, but these folks seemed convinced I should do it, and in the absence of any clear sense of what I wanted to do with my life, I enrolled in real estate classes.

The same week I passed the exam and received my sales-person license, I quit my job at the association. Suddenly, I no longer had anyone telling me when to show up, what to do, and when I could leave. This really felt like freedom!

I also quit college. I'd mentally quit college after the first year and stopped going to class. I remember getting academic suspension warning letters because I wasn't doing any of the work, but I was like "Screw college." I'm an important real estate agent now. I didn't mention this part to my parents. I only told them when they wanted to know why I wasn't asking for help with the next semester's tuition. Was I doing so well in real estate that I didn't need their financial aid? Nope. Despite not having a paycheck, not being enrolled in school, and not making a sale, I didn't care. I felt free.

Freedom Drives Human Behavior

Would you agree that freedom is one of the most dominant drivers of human behavior?

Almost everything we do is designed to lead to ever-increasing amounts of freedom. Some people get multiple degrees because they believe they'll lead to a high-paying job and will free them from worries about money.

In the not-too-distant past, people would work for several decades at the same company because they believed that when they retired, they'd have enough money to experience ultimate freedom as they checked items off their bucket list. Those with an entrepreneurial spirit work hard to build a business because they believe it will provide them enough money and freedom to live the lifestyle they have decided they want. In each case, people are working hard to earn money because money equals freedom, right?

Not so fast. You know that's not true.

We can look around and see plenty of examples of people who feel trapped by their high-paying jobs. Often I'd watch these people get into real estate once they'd built up enough courage to leave that "safe job" with a regular paycheck. At that point, their desire for freedom to control their own schedule had grown larger than their desire for the perceived safety of a regular paycheck. They'd start their career in real estate with the same feeling of ultimate freedom that I had. Sadly, the few who make it and become successful eventually feel even more trapped than when they were an employee.

When you're new in the real estate business, you quickly learn who the top producers are. They're the people who are always running between appointments with clients, never in the office for long, and get all the monthly awards. To a newbie, it seems like they have it all, money and freedom. Then one day you hear them talking about how they have no life.

Wait, what?

To the ears of the newly licensed agent, that sounds rather shocking, disconcerting even. How can it be that these people have both money and the freedom to do what they want, when they want, and still say they have no life?

First, as many business owners already know (and real estate sales is very much a business), a lot happens between the top and bottom lines of a profit-and-loss statement. Just because there is money coming in doesn't mean there are substantial profits. This is important because so many people go into business for themselves, looking for control over both their income and their time.

In fact, the most common answer when real estate brokers ask a new agent why they want to get into the business, they say they like houses, want to control their own schedule, and want to help people. If they were being honest with themselves, they'd say they want to make a lot of money, but for fear of being judged, rarely bring that up.

Looking back, I'm grateful I got to observe this dynamic from inside the real estate industry at such an early age. While my peers were partying in college, I was already in the middle of some intense professional growth.

The desire to have direct control over income and time extends beyond real estate agents.

Eventually, I learned that self-employed people across all industries often mistake impulsive behavior for freedom. Especially when a person shifts from a highly structured corporate environment to one where they have more direct control over their day, they almost immediately give in to their impulses. With little thought to the consequences of their actions, they live in the moment and do what feels pleasurable and easy. They haven't yet learned that often the best move for their career is doing the task that feels difficult.

You can see this when kids go off to college and temporarily get off track because they've lost the structure imposed by high school and living with their parents. It takes a while for them to learn what to do with this newfound freedom. At least they have the university system to provide some structure. And you can certainly see it when people go from a traditional office environment to a work-from-home model or into business for themselves. When the structure provided by working in the office in a corporate setting is gone, even mature adults have to go through an adjustment.

Our culture still largely lives for 5:00 p.m. and the weekend where we can let our guard down and give in to our impulses, which isn't bad because we all need to relax and let off steam. The problem is that the world doesn't reward individuals who continually allow their impulses to push them around. It doesn't reward those who have no discipline over their mind and, thus their thoughts and feelings. Doing what you want, when you want, is fine as long as it's balanced with times of discipline and structure.

That was the first profound lesson I remember learning as a teenage self-employed real estate agent. Whereas most of the adults around me got into the business to have more control over their schedule, it was obvious even to me they exercised little control over anything. That's why most failed. I should say it again: that's why most failed. No one taught them how to work, and because of that, they failed.

But I observed a few people who were both top producers and seemed to have a life. To control (your schedule) is a verb and the most successful people in my office pushed aside their impulses and took conscious control over their actions. There was even a pattern.

Do What Successful People Do

By the time I'd get to my real estate office around 9:00 (or 9:30) in the morning with my pumpkin scone and venti mocha frappuccino from Starbucks, these successful people were already hard at work. At that age, I was driven by a desire to prove I could make something out of myself without a college degree, so I decided the best thing to do was mimic their schedule. I started getting to the office early, and before long, my competitive spirit kicked in and my goal was to get there first.

What I saw was a small group of focused people who were doing all the sales-generating techniques the other agents whined about—namely, prospecting and scheduling appointments. By the time the other agents got to the office and got sort of serious about work, these successful folks were done.

The person who sticks out in my mind clearly to this day is my friend Kelly. She wasn't my friend then. I felt too intimidated to talk to her. She was a single mom who was not in the office for social hour. My desk was serendipitously next to hers, and I watched as she steadily built momentum from the moment she sat down.

She would typically start by taking care of some easy paperwork or by doing other admin work. Then she'd transition into reading positive affirmations and what looked to me at the time like a short meditation on her financial goals. She had a few index cards stuck to the wall of her cubicle right in front of her eyes that listed her big goals with the amount of money needed to achieve them. Then when the clock struck 9:00, she would pick up the phone and call her new leads, past clients, and anyone she could to start conversations and generate appointments.

Around 1:00 p.m. each day, she would head out on those appointments until it was time to pick up her son from school. This was a daily habit. I'm sure there were days she'd give in to her impulses to break from her discipline, but that didn't happen often. In fact, it was so infrequent I can't remember a single instance. Not every successful person I observed in those days was a single mom, obviously. They all had different situations in their personal lives, but they had one important trait in common. They were done with their most important work by midday. This fascinated me because I couldn't find any specific training or coaching they had in common, and our broker never discussed this in sales meetings. In Kelly's case, generating leads and setting appointments with prospective clients was always at the top of her list. Of course, when you work for yourself in any industry, the basics of salesmanship will always be the most important work.

Conversely, most of the agents who were hanging around the office in the afternoon without clients were always struggling. So, even though I didn't have many (or any) clients, I followed the lead of the top producers. I wasn't always sure what I should do at first, but I made my best guess and worked on disciplining myself to finish whatever it was I thought I should do by 1:00 in the afternoon. Somehow, I knew that in the long run, establishing that pattern was far more important than mastering any specific task.

Eventually, my business picked up. As I took on clients, I got busy. Not necessarily productive, but definitely busy. Okay, let me stop lying. I had like two clients, and suddenly I felt like the busiest person on earth. Feeling busy is incredibly addictive, and when you're starting from nothing, any activity feels like progress.

One major downside to busy work is that it allows a person to hide from challenging but important work that must get done. If I didn't feel like prospecting, I'd catch myself getting absorbed in busy work. And this was before the internet. There's a limit to what two clients needed from me, so I imagine I would clean my desk, sort papers, see if there were donuts in the breakroom, and mindlessly talk to another agent looking for the same excuse not to prospect.

This is when I learned the pattern I'd observed wasn't easy to imitate. I was totally blindsided by my own fears and hesitations that were triggered by my initial attempts to self-impose just a tiny bit of structure. My goal: follow Kelly's lead and get my prospecting Done Before One.

That was the goal, and the second a client or two fell into my lap, I fell flat on my face. I experienced doubt, fear of failure, criticism, and impostor syndrome. The top producers around me rarely seemed engaged in busy work, so I assumed they had conquered their fears. In order to conquer mine, I hired a coach.

The specific coaching program that came through my company at the time was also a predestined event. Remember, since this was real estate, I obviously learned how to sell, but my coach also insisted that I learn how to manage my time. In a nutshell, he taught me that spending the money I'd earn would not be enjoyable if I didn't learn how to spend my time. This made sense, given I'd just observed successful agents in my company who'd gotten stuck in that exact predicament.

Over the years, through continuous work with my coach and a lot of trial and error, I built a way of moving through the day that allowed me to stay focused in the morning and have flexibility and freedom in the afternoon. Although I didn't think of it this way when I was doing it, I formulated an answer to the question of how to work. I'd designed my own lifestyle.

As our world has sped up, we've become obsessed with perfecting the daily schedule. Each time I come across another book or journal about the perfect routine, I find an overly complicated system that seems hell-bent on accounting for every second of the day and wrestling it to the ground, forcing every reader into that author's exact style.

You can see it in the way these books and journals are marketed. Headlines like, "Copy my exact system for the perfect daily routine" are everywhere. Even those focused primarily on the mornings (win the morning, win the day!) expand into an overwhelming and rigid daily system.

I suppose it's human nature to want to find a routine that works and copy it. It's what I did initially, but the problem is people aren't the same. The perfect daily routine doesn't exist beyond a single individual. But that doesn't stop people from continuing to look. I've seen those who cycle through several planning systems in one year and never commit to any of them. Often, when you see people doing that, they use the search itself as an excuse not to tackle the real productive work they are afraid of doing—or are intimidated by, rather than finding a system that works.

The truth is all systems, even the complicated ones, work if you use them. But I believe what people are really looking for is a method that they can use to design their own lifestyle, just as I did. The key is to use principles to build a lifestyle that works for you.

That's what this book is about—the principles and a method for your own powerful answer for how to work when you work for yourself. As long as you're able to confront your fears along the way, this will be the last book on productivity you'll need. But I almost didn't write it.

2

THE 10 ESSENTIAL DONE BEFORE ONE PRINCIPLES

Find the discipline to do the activities you resist,
like prospecting by 1:00 p.m. each day.
Then let go. Who cares what happens after that?

Recently, one of my favorite podcasts dedicated an episode to yet another discussion on the perfect daily routine. The podcast host himself has given interviews about his own routine for other podcasts and has extensively written about it on his blog. Yet he was raving about this fresh approach he'd heard of and couldn't wait for us to hear the interview with the guy who'd impressed him. I had a hunch that there wouldn't be a groundbreaking new approach, but I decided to listen regardless.

These two geeked out for an hour over morning routines, then ran out of time. So the podcast host allowed the guest to self-record the parts of his routine they hadn't gone through, and he tacked another hour onto the backend of this episode. The guest went into excruciating detail about his morning journaling, red light therapy, cold plunge, breakfast (including how he cooked it, how his family participated), when he would go to the gym, when he took a shower and on and on and on. His morning routine was so complex he didn't even sit down to work until 11:30 a.m. I mean, come on, dude.

Is he serious? If I did everything he described, I'd be exhausted by 11:30 in the morning. I came away from the episode in disbelief that he actually did this so-called perfect routine every day, and even if he did, you can't convince me he's doing his best work when his stomach is likely demanding lunch. Then I wondered, do people really want to hear this? Why do I keep bumping into podcasts and blogs about people's daily routines?

Why does this have to be so complicated?

The day after I heard the podcast, I received a text message from one of my longtime clients who said, "Spending our #donebeforeone day clearing land after the storm!" What she meant was that she was enjoying the freedom to spend the afternoon working on her property guilt-free, and without sacrificing her professional productivity, because she'd already accomplished the most important tasks in her business during the morning hours.

On that day, it clicked. Self-employed people searching for the perfect morning routine are looking for an integrated approach to get work done efficiently and empower them to enjoy other areas of their lives. In other words, the search for the morning routine is the search for the freedoms many think show up automatically when you work for yourself.

I've spent many years working to teach thousands of self-employed people how to take positive control of their time. You see, after selling homes for thirteen years, I became a sales coach and sometimes I had to trick my students into success. So to get them to do the jobs they resisted, which were the important tasks they needed to do to succeed, I'd issue a challenge: find the discipline to do the activities you resist, like prospecting by 1:00 p.m. each day. Then let go. Who cares what happens after that? Go home. Go shopping. Go to the movies. Go on a three-hour lunch. Whatever. Just control the day until 1:00 p.m.

Of course, I knew what would happen if they took me up on that challenge because years ago I'd lived it myself. Eventually, they would start generating clients and wouldn't be able to screw off each afternoon. Instead, they'd have to go on appointments, which is, of course, what they wanted. It became known as the Done Before One challenge. I never thought of it that way when I was younger, simply doing my best to mimic the top producers around me. It only became a "thing" because I needed a clever way to persuade my students. Over time, the concept expanded into a more complete answer to the question "How do I work when I work for myself?" and it's guided by this set of ten principles:

1. **Control the day until 1:00 p.m.**
   This is the primary guiding principle. When you control the first part of your day, you accomplish more than you ever thought possible. Before your competition even finishes lunch, you'll have outproduced them and will be free to continue work or move on to other activities guilt-free.

2. **Control your inputs.**
   Inputs for our purposes are anything you focus your attention on, or that gets your attention, and triggers thought. In life, you get what you think about, whether you want it or not, so taking control of your inputs is critical to success. The way to control your inputs is to take responsibility for where you place your attention. When you feel negative emotions such as fear, doubt, and worry, it's a signal that it's time to edit your inputs by redirecting your attention.

3. **Treat every task as an appointment.**
   Everything we do in life takes time. We have 1,440 minutes to spend each day, and how we spend them is more important than how we spend our money. Time-blocking tasks in your calendar and honoring your commitments to those appointments is another big key to success. If it's not on your calendar, it doesn't exist.

4. **Finish the day before it begins.**
Never go into a workday unsure about what to do. Determining what you'll do during the first half of the next day, in advance, provides long-term freedom of time.

5. **Produce before you consume.**
When you're self-employed, your primary job is to generate leads and that task always comes before all others. From there, you must prioritize tasks within projects that will grow the business and deliver for current customers. You must finish these things for the day before you can safely begin consuming content others have produced.

6. **Take one full day off each week.**
Taking time to fully recharge at regular intervals is critical to success. When you're burned out and still working, you're a danger to the client and to your own health. Once you demonstrate a pattern of showing up fully rested and sharp, your clients will respect your day off.

7. **Don't do busy.**
Carrying around busy energy is a sign you can't handle your life. It's a scarcity-based signal to the universe that you don't want more. Top performers don't do busy. Instead, they consciously make choices about how they spend their time with a focus placed on activities that advance them toward their goals.

8. **Don't use words against yourself.**
Negative self-talk is more destructive than all the criticism offered from the world, and there will always be

plenty of that. There is no honor in beating yourself up. Do your honest best and move on.

9. **Accept accountability as an inside job.**
   No one can hold you accountable for your dreams and goals except you. When you are clear about what you want, accountability is automatic. When you find yourself seeking accountability, you are actually seeking clarity of desire.

10. **Know your Big Why.**
    You aren't your profession. Through your work, you serve others, and because of that you attract abundance, which is used to fund your life. Your career exists as a servant to your Big Why.

You can realize the freedoms you seek as a self-employed business owner and entrepreneur by applying these ten principles to your daily life. If you want to enjoy the freedom to work where you want, when you want, with whom you want, and on what you want, a little structure and discipline is in order. Not 24/7 military-style discipline, but enough that you have deliberate control over the first half of the day.

I've learned from coaching thousands of professionals over the last two decades that most people reading this are excited by the idea of being done with work by 1:00 p.m., but are wondering how it's even possible. If you're normal, you might initially struggle to see how such a strategy could work for you.

Additionally, you're highly likely to be met with resistance when you try to apply the method to your daily life. That's why I took what I pieced together for myself to succeed as a business owner and formalized it for my students and private clients. Now, as you work your way through the book, you can implement the Done Before One method into your life at your own pace. You'll see the ten principles we just covered showing up all over the rest of the book. Challenge yourself as you read to connect the tactics you discover to the principles.

To get you ready to fully receive the tactics that you'll use to build your own Done Before One lifestyle, we need to work on two important skills: controlling your time and your focus.

3

RECLAIM YOUR TIME AND FOCUS

You're not too busy, and you're not overwhelmed, but you may be unfocused and leaking huge amounts of time.

Don't Do Busy

Everyone is so busy, have you noticed? If I ask a high-producing salesperson how they're doing, they'll likely say, "Great but I'm so busy!" If I ask a low-producing salesperson how they are doing, they'll certainly admit business could be better, then tell me they're just so busy it's hard to find time to prospect. Busy doing what you ask? Tapping and scrolling, perhaps?

It's not just salespeople either. Everyone seems to walk around these days with a badge on their chest labeled "busy." This is not something to be proud of because, while truly effective people may be busy, they aren't constantly in that state, and they definitely don't boast about it.

Having a full calendar isn't the same thing as walking around with busy energy. Busy energy is a smokescreen for those trying to cover up their weaknesses. Busy energy is a cover for those who don't know how to use their calendar to help them spend their time. Busy is cover for a person who can't set and hold boundaries, who is fearful of change, who is unwilling to face deeper emotional wounds, who is addicted to the adrenaline rush of always being on or who isn't willing to face issues at home.

Worse, when someone has a habit of professing how busy they are, that busy energy is broadcast to those around them and to life itself, which hears: "I can't handle what I have on my plate right now so please don't bring me anymore." The problem with this is that most people I know still want more out of life but are unaware they are blocking it themselves.

- Why would life, or your boss, or prospective clients give you more to handle when you can't shut up about how overwhelmed you are with what you've already got?
- Why would your friends want to invite you to fun events when you've conditioned them to think you're always too busy?
- Why would your family and pets want to be around you, unless they have to?

If I'm talking about you, listen up. You're not too busy and you're not overwhelmed, but you may be unfocused and leaking huge amounts of time. I have yet to meet someone who enjoys living life this way. Even if it's a subconscious knowing, we all instinctively understand it's not healthy to carry around busy energy. One big key to living a Done Before One lifestyle is deciding to drop the busy badge.

Reclaim Your Time

Another key to positive change is learning to reclaim your time. I can't hear the words *reclaiming* and *time* without thinking of the hilarious congressional scene in the summer of 2017 when Representative Maxine Waters was grilling an individual testifying at a hearing who kept deflecting her questions by making flattering remarks. She picked up on it and would cut the gentleman off by loudly proclaiming, "reclaiming my time." The two went around in circles in a word sparring match, and by the end she'd said that phrase so many times it broke through the news cycle and turned into a comical meme that spread through social media like wildfire.

Prior to this interaction, unless you were a student of parliamentary procedure, you likely had no clue what that phrase meant. In parliamentary procedure, the chairperson assigns speakers a specific amount of time to address a topic. If the speaker finishes early, they can yield the balance of their time to others, *but they still own that time*, which means they can take it back before it runs out. When a congressional representative reclaims their time, they are literally taking back something that belongs to them in that environment.

But if you think about it, doesn't your time always belong to you? I've never spoken to an audience that didn't agree that time is far more valuable than money. Yet some people penny-pinch their way through life to save money while wasting huge amounts of time tapping and scrolling through social media, just to name one example.

When working with people, it's important to pay more attention to what they do than what they say. If you really want to learn what a person values and what they fear, watch their actions. This applies to ourselves too. If we say that time is more valuable than money, and that our time always belongs to us, then we can become more intentional in how we spend our time.

You deserve to live a good life, and even though the unfolding of that life won't always be perfect, even though adversity always comes with growth, you can learn to choose happiness. You can learn how to reclaim the time and energy you've been giving away to others or let it slowly leak away as you stare at glowy rectangles (this image seems obvious, but I'm referring to that smartphone that's sitting next to you).

I've never seen a trophy for the best workaholic, and no one I've ever been around who was critically ill gave a shit about their email or anything else on the internet for that matter. In fact, in *The Top Five Regrets of the Dying* by Bronnie Ware, three of the regrets people list are wishing they'd had the courage to live the life they wanted instead of what others expected of them, that they hadn't worked so hard, and that they let themselves be happier.

If you don't want to end up on your deathbed with those specific regrets, you're going to have to get serious about reclaiming your time and designing a life that you truly want to live. Paying attention to how you spend your time helps you reclaim it.

How Would You Spend 1,440 Minutes?

One of my favorite visuals ever created is the Life Calendar by Wait But Why blog founder Tim Urban. If you haven't seen it, picture a large poster with nothing but rows of blocks. There are ninety rows of blocks; each block represents a week, and each row represents one year of your life. Coloring it to your present age is a modern day way to make the same point as the ancient phrase *memento mori*. It's effective symbolism for sure.

What I like about the poster is that it requires active participation to have the most meaning. Looking at a skull to help you remember the impermanence of life is one thing. Ticking off the weeks of your life one by one, never knowing if you'll get to mark off another box, is another. But for the purposes of the Done Before One lifestyle, there's another more immediately useful metric to consider and that's the total number of minutes in a day. Each day has 1,440 minutes and while it's great to ponder your own death to help you stay present, raising your awareness of the minutes in the day can help you make the most of your time right now, moment to moment. Has anyone ever approached you and said, "Hey do you have a minute?" Happens all the time doesn't it? What did you do the last time that happened?

If you're normal, you stopped what you were doing and gave this person your attention. In effect, you gave that person the most valuable thing you have to give—your attention and your time. Here's the kicker: you gave them time whether you should have or not, whether they deserved it or not.

This is a common occurrence in daily life for a number of reasons. First, it feels good to help someone out. When someone asks if you have a minute, there's a good chance they need help with something and think highly enough about you to ask for your help. That provides a quick boost to the ego.

Second, when you divert your attention, you get momentary relief from stress. For example, if you were doing something that wasn't your favorite task to do, like accounting or prospecting, then the person who approached you has provided a perfect excuse to stop.

Third is reciprocity. Human beings are hard-wired to understand the concept of reciprocity. If you stop and help the person, it's assumed that one day they will return the favor.

None of this is bad, per se. But you have to consider what the effect of consistently diverting your attention is having on your overall life. The University of California, Irvine conducted a widely published study that showed each interruption takes a person an average of 23 minutes and 15 seconds to refocus on their previous task. They noted one exception when the interruption aligned perfectly with what you were working on. In that case, the interruption can be helpful, but use your instincts here. How many times are interruptions actually about the thing you're focused on?

Do You Have a Minute?

So when someone approaches you and asks if you have a minute, what they're really asking for is 23 minutes and 15 seconds PLUS whatever time it takes to listen to their issue and respond. Let's pretend each interruption takes 10 minutes. Seems harmless, right? I mean, what's 10 minutes? Well, I know you're good enough with math to know it's really 33 minutes. When someone tells me they're so busy and having a hard time getting things done, this is the first problem I think of. At 33 minutes per interruption, it doesn't take many to throw off an entire day.

Speaking of an entire day, using our example, you could be interrupted 43.6 times before you hit the total of 1,440 minutes in a day. But are you really interrupted that many times? It turns out, people aren't the only (or even the biggest) source of interruptions. As of 2023, Reviews.org determined the average person checks their phone 144 times per day. That's once every 10 minutes.

I recently had a client struggling to make meaningful progress with a team that had a bad habit of showing up for every meeting unfocused and unprepared and having made no progress since the last meeting. Her frustration comes from the fact that she was hired as a consultant to help them win a multi-billion-dollar grant, and she could tell they were likely to blow it if their behavior didn't change. Exasperated, one day she asked me if I thought people were really that distracted and confused. I mean, isn't $5 billion enough to make a person super dialed in? Do they not care she wondered?

I suggested it wasn't that they didn't care. As she described how stressed and frantic they were behaving, it was obvious to me they cared deeply about winning this grant. But they needed help. When you combine human interruptions with technology interruptions, the team she was trying to guide likely never experienced one moment in the day when they were undistracted, in flow, and producing their best work.

Instead, their workday was pretty much an endless cycle of emails, meetings, waiting for others to return emails, waiting for others to make decisions, more emails and meetings, breaks, lunches, social media distractions, and so on.

Sound even a little familiar? Such is the modern workday. No wonder people feel stressed.

It's far too easy to get stuck in an unproductive loop where you feel busy, but on some level know you're just chasing your tail. All of this isn't intentional. No one goes into work with the explicit goal of being ineffective. But unless you have a superb mentor or pursue the knowledge yourself, no one in the standard Western school system teaches us how to get shit done in life.

But as the saying goes, you have the same amount of minutes in the day that Madonna has, so what's the excuse? Madonna may have more money, but she doesn't have more minutes in the day than anyone else. Could the difference in wealth be more about how she spends her minutes rather than her dollars?

Think of it this way: when was the last time you worked diligently to save money on a purchase? Or the opposite: when was the last time you beat yourself up for spending too much on something frivolous? We've all been guilty of worrying more about our money than our time. Honestly, which has more value to you?

If you're younger, say in your twenties, you may be tempted to answer with money. I suppose we all think that way when we're younger, but the problem is in assuming we'll live a long, healthy life. I hope you do, but the older you get, the more you realize you just never know. Sadly, I've worked with people from all age ranges who put more value on money than time. Sometimes death has to affect us close to home before we wake up.

But if I've even for a moment caused you to consider that time is infinitely more valuable, then we can get on with some life-changing work. You see, you'd never allow someone to steal your money, and when time is even more valuable to you, you'll stop allowing people and outside influences, like social media, to steal your time.

The best way to do this is to get out of any kind of victim-based mindset. Just as a smart financial adviser would encourage you to take responsibility for your finances, so you're less likely to be taken advantage of, I'm encouraging you to take responsibility for how you spend your time. Here's the hard truth: no one or no thing can interrupt you, but you can interrupt yourself.

Unplug from the Matrix

Yet another key to the Done Before One lifestyle is unplugging from the matrix. There was a time when reclaiming your time used to be as simple as keeping a log of how you were spending your time. If for a period of one week you were to write down what you did each day in thirty-minute increments, it would become clear which tasks you should weed out to reclaim your time and regain your focus. But today, all of us have allowed ourselves to be sucked into the social media matrix and have wasted embarrassingly large amounts of time.

If you're old enough to have been in the workforce pre-smartphone days, you know what I mean. Because of technology's broken promise, we now have a couple generations of people who don't know the peace of walking around outside and actually observing life around themselves. We've become zombies who've learned to walk around while staring at our glowy rectangles without veering into the street and getting run over.

I've started to divide my own life in some interesting ways: pre-email and post-email pre-iPhone and post-iPhone, pre–social media and post–social media. Prior to social media, I never had much of a problem with productivity. Because I started in commission-only sales at eighteen years old, early on I developed a heightened awareness of both the value of time and how humans behaved in different situations.

Friendster.com was my first social media experience. The next was a very brief time on Myspace before going all in on Facebook. By the time we had apps, I'd become distracted and my attention was being splintered all over the place. Like everyone, I fell for the trap, but I think it was my salesmanship skills that allowed me to see what was happening.

One morning while waiting for my latte at the end of the counter in Starbucks, I noticed everyone around me was staring into their glowy rectangles waiting for their drinks too. No one was talking except to place their order. In fact, some people were holding their devices up almost as a shield. They folded their right arm across their midsection, rested their left elbow on the wrist of their right arm, and held the phone out in front of them with their left hand. You've seen this posture, haven't you? Well, to me, it looked like the way people held the phone was like a shield. This nonverbal communication was screaming, "Don't approach me! Don't you dare come say hi to a stranger!"

Of course, just because I observed this didn't mean I wasn't guilty of the same behavior. I spent years working to break my addiction to my device and will probably always have to be vigilant about not getting sucked back in. But it was the months after the pandemic that strengthened my resolve to think beyond the phone itself and make a genuine commitment to unplugging from the matrix. During that time, I lived in California, and as you may know, or have experienced personally, daily life was night and day different from other states like Texas or Florida. With everything else so disrupted, I became more addicted to my glowy rectangle than at any other time.

I've never been addicted to any substances, but I imagine that the constant dopamine hits mixed with a sense of hopelessness would feel similar. This went on for longer than I want to admit. After the shock of my dog Chug!'s transition, I feel like I experienced a moment of grace. I had a strong desire to get back to the level of happiness and fulfillment I had experienced pre-iPhone. I needed a digital detox.

Try a Digital Detox

As I'm sure you know, the idea behind a digital detox is to reduce the constant stimulation of dopamine in the brain to help you regain mindfulness, improve your sleep, and even lower your blood pressure. There's an argument in the scientific community over whether this actually works because our bodies are always producing some dopamine. Just because you stop using your smartphone doesn't mean you'll detox from dopamine. Excessive eating or drinking can produce the same effect in the brain as a smartphone addiction.

While we leave the debate on neurotransmitters to the scientists, we can certainly agree that if we don't reign in our digital lives, we'll continue to struggle with having enough time and focusing on anything meaningful. The task at hand, then, is to give our minds space.

The older I get, the more I understand the value of creating space in all areas of our lives. When I'm coaching private clients, I'm not telling them what to do as much as I am holding the space for them to arrive at their own solution.

We can learn how to work out and lose weight online, but we hire personal trainers because they hold the space for us to actually do the work. We can read self-help books to improve our relationships, but we go to a therapist because of the space they hold for us to work on highly emotional issues.

Everywhere you look, you can see how holding space for each other and for ourselves is a lost secret to happiness, joy, and the life we want. I can't think of anything more adept at crowding out space than the content streaming through our glowy rectangles.

Creating space is simple, but not easy. I'm not an addiction specialist, but I know that each of us will reach a point where we've had enough and will seek ways to build space back into our lives. Here are a few ways to build space into your own life:

- Turn off all notifications on your phone.
- Set your screen to black and white to avoid being drawn in by the vibrant colors.
- Use the time-limiting features on social media apps.
- Practice running errands without your phone.
- Go on walks without your phone or turn it to Airplane Mode if you're counting steps. It doesn't need a signal to count steps.
- Put your phone on a charger after dinner and walk away.
- Consider eliminating the phone for one full day each week. Sunday has worked best for me.

One change from that list has recently made a big difference in my own life. For years, I'd use my afternoon walks to catch up on podcasts and audiobooks, and of course I'd mindlessly tap and scroll if I wasn't in the mood to listen to audio. But lately I've been switching the phone to Airplane Mode.

Those afternoon walks are meant to help me put work away and transition to other parts of my life. The problem is that my mind was not getting the space it needed to process all the other inputs it received throughout the day. Constantly cramming your mind with other people's thoughts does nothing but crowd out your own.

I understand the desire to use every minute productively, but sometimes the most productive act you can do is give your mind space. It can seem counterintuitive, but when you relax and let your mind wander on its own, just this pensive act can lead you to thoughts, ideas, and solutions to problems that seem magical.

No doubt you've solved some of your biggest problems in the shower. Runners know they'll hit a certain point in their run where their mind lets go and they'll start generating all kinds of creative ideas and solutions. Unplugging from your digital life will deliver the same results.

Redirect Your Focus

Now, finally, you have space to redirect your focus. When your mind has space, reclaiming your time makes it easier to direct your focus. But I've noticed it's not obvious to everyone where their focus should be placed.

Through your chosen career, you serve others and for that you receive money, which can then be used to live a great life. On a very basic level, that means you can live the life you want. You only need to determine how many people you must serve to generate the income required. Understanding that simple premise alone can be transformational—especially for salespeople and self-employed business owners.

Getting anything you want in life becomes a function of determining how much the thing you want costs, then establishing how many people you must help in order to have the money for it. In order to serve the required number of people, you must develop a habit of directing your focus, if only at key times during the day, and it won't surprise you when I say that key time is before 1:00 p.m.

No matter what your daily life looks like, most agree we get about 80 percent of our results from roughly 20 percent of the actions we take. This agreement comes from the remarkable accuracy of the Pareto Principle (the 80/20 rule) introduced in the late 1800s by Italian sociologist Vilfredo Pareto. One of his earliest observations was that about 80 percent of the land in Italy was owned by roughly 20 percent of the population. Then he found other countries had the same distribution pattern.

Fast-forward to today and you can see this principle everywhere. Roughly 20 percent of salespeople produce 80 percent of the sales, 20 percent of clients produce 80 percent of the revenues, 20 percent of patients incur 80 percent of health-care-related expenses, and even tech companies know that fixing the top 20 percent of reported bugs eliminates 80 percent of problems and crashes in their software.

But it's not important to get hung up on exact numbers. There's enough evidence in the world that when you direct your focus to the 20 percent of tasks that deliver most of your results, you're much more likely to thrive and live a life you truly enjoy.

As a business owner or salesperson—and really what's the difference—your 20 percent comes from prospecting and sales activities. This is where you should direct your focus during the first half of the day, at a minimum. Specifically, you should set your daily focus on tasks that push you toward your quarterly sales and income goals. Then, if you set your quarterly goals based on your yearly goal, you're set.

Out of all the activities you do in a day, with all this time you've reclaimed, I want you to be crystal clear that the most important 20 percent of your activities are those that cause you to generate leads and make sales. That's how you keep your family from worrying and your own mind at ease. If you think about it, none of this matters if you aren't making sales, so to an extent I've been assuming all along that you have solid marketing campaigns set up that are bringing you enough leads to make the sales you need to make. If that's not the case for you, then you must use every minute of time you've reclaimed to learn those skills.

My first book teaches everything you need to know about sales, but it's written for residential real estate agents. If you're willing to put up with some industry talk and do some translating for your own profession, I'm certain it will help you. It's called *The Top Producer Life: Build the Real Estate Career of Your Dreams in Any Economy*. Maybe one day I'll write a book on sales and marketing mastery for everyone. But for now, if I were your sales manager and only had a few paragraphs to help you, I'd say this:

- **Your database (email list) is your business.** These days, everyone has loads of competition and the consumer has all the power. While you may have other assets with value in your business, your most valuable asset is your relationship with your database of current and past customers and all the data you've collected about them over the years. That being the case, make sure you formalize this asset.

  Gather all the data and compile it into a single software program. Categorize everyone and track all the activities and conversations you have with them. Never let an interaction with your client pass without recording what happened. Remembering minor details from the past will shock your customers (because no one else does) and will build loyalty fast.

Also, remember to be patient. Building a robust database takes time. You may start out with only a person's email address and a year later have their full name, physical address, phone number, birthday, kid and pet names, kid and pet birthdays, credit card number, favorite restaurant, and so on.

- **Marketing and sales are not the same thing.** Marketing helps build brand awareness, it helps generate leads, and it can strengthen your relationship with past customers. Sales is guiding people who need your product or service now to a place where they feel comfortable making a decision to hire you. Eventually, you'll need to be good at both.

- **Use two primary ways to generate leads.** One is active and the other is passive. In a healthy business, both methods are utilized, but if you're just starting out, you may need to begin with active lead generation. This is old-school prospecting and includes cold calling, warm calling, individual emails, direct messages, and in-person conversations like networking and door knocking. The best in every industry still use these tactics, even the phone.

  Do not let anyone tell you the phone doesn't work to generate leads. There isn't time to sell you on why in this book, so I trust you understand I'm never going to say something that would cause you to have less business. In any case, when you're just starting out, you aren't going to have a huge marketing budget, so until you do, this style of active lead generation is what you'll do.

  Then, as you build up some reserves, you'll be able to experiment with passive lead generation. That's what

everyone else calls marketing. I label it as passive because once you place your ads, you have to sit back and
wait to see if anyone responds to them. Ultimately, you
can leverage this kind of marketing because entire firms
specialize in running online ad campaigns and can do it
better than you. And that's okay because it'll leave you
time to stay focused on what no one can do better than
you: staying connected on a human level to the people
you serve, also known as active lead generation.

- **Think of referrals in reverse.** Most people think they
receive referrals because the person sending the referral is trying to help them. But they are actually trying
to help themselves. The hidden secret in all referrals
is that the person recommending you is only doing so
because they believe you will make them look good. If
they think there is even a chance of you underperforming, they'll hold back.

   If you want more referrals, remember to communicate to your database that it's safe to refer you. And not
only that it's safe, that it's one of your primary goals to
make them look like a hero when they do refer you.

- **World-class salespeople master the conversion chain.**
Generating leads is one thing, but if you don't know what
to do with them, you're sunk. The chain can begin with a
phone call, but these days usually starts with digital communication like an email or DM inquiry. Your only goal at
that point is to convert the lead to a phone call. Once on
the phone, your only goal is to convert them to a proper
sales appointment. During the appointment, you search
for a problem they have that your product or service can
solve and you close for the business. Digital to voice, to

appointment to client. That's the chain, and if you focus on one step at a time, your performance will steadily improve.

- **Getting good at selling comes in three stages.** First, your only goal is to build momentum. Talk to as many people as you can about what you do. Prospect like a maniac and go on as many appointments as you can. Once you build up a critical amount of momentum, you'll can work on your skills. That's the second stage and eventually leads to mastery where you learn the only skills to work on over and over until the day you retire are the basics.

To summarize this chapter, when you don't let yourself get overwhelmed by the less important busywork (the other 80 percent), you will discover that you have ample time for the work that truly matters, including the capacity to handle unexpected challenges and opportunities that will inevitably arise.

Reclaiming your time and then redirecting your focus can cause a profound mindset shift. When a person empowers themselves to take control of their actions and is then shown how to do it, their productivity in life increases. Salespeople make more sales, leaders produce better teams, artists produce better creative works, parents raise better children, and all of this improved production comes with an improved sense of self-worth.

It's the opposite of busy energy. As your sense of self-worth improves, so does your overall mood. Anxiety falls away along with all the self-imposed stressful thoughts, and life becomes more fun. This is important not just because of your own mental and physical health, but because you are a mentor to someone. We all serve as a mentor, it's just that some do it intentionally. Unless you isolate yourself from other humans entirely, you have family, friends, coworkers, and even pets who are observing you, and they can sense your energy when you are around them.

So you have to ask yourself, do you want the people and animals you cherish most to sense your busy energy, or would you prefer them to perceive a person who is centered and happy? Would you prefer them to watch you struggle to carve out time for them or to feel special and loved because they have your undivided attention? Would you prefer your children to grow up and mimic your busy energy or would you rather they grow up watching someone handle life with skill and grace and feel inspired to do the same?

Ultimately, you are responsible for the energy you bring to the room and for consciously directing your attention. You'll get nowhere playing the victim. The individuals (including pets) in your life deserve your undivided attention. Your career and your hobbies deserve your undivided attention. And your mind needs space to plug into sources for inspiration and guidance.

In the next chapter, I dive right into the how-to of the routine. As you implement the Done Before One practice in your daily life, you'll see ample opportunities to live by the concepts I've covered so far. Before long, you'll encounter the resistance I mentioned in the form of self-doubt, limiting beliefs, criticisms from others who notice your changes, and even skepticism from clients and prospects. When this happens, it's a positive sign you're making progress and Part II of the book will help you grow through that resistance.

It's not hard to learn how to create your own Done Before One lifestyle. To be sure, this is not rocket science, and you may even encounter variations of ideas you've heard of before. The hard part is working through the resistance until you not only understand the philosophy academically, but are living it daily. When that happens, you know your mind has transferred the knowledge to the body, and it's become an unconscious part of who you are.

Now, since there's clearly so much interest in the morning routine, turn the page and let's get to it.

4

HOW TO BUILD YOUR OWN MORNING ROUTINE

The purpose of the morning routine is to take control of, and build momentum into, your day. That's it.

Build Your Morning Routine

I want to put this concept of the morning routine into perspective so you never again have to waste time picking apart anyone else's. There is no perfect morning routine that works for everyone. That means you can stop looking.

It also means if you continue to look, you're likely using the search as an excuse not to decide on what you will do each morning to get into action and go after your goals. Further, if you ever copy a routine created by someone else and then make no progress toward your goals, this failure becomes an easy scapegoat from taking personal responsibility.

Who you are today is not who you'll be in the future. You'll continue to grow as a human being, your professional goals will change, and that will cause you to want to make adjustments to your routines. If you create your own routine around a set of guidelines that allows for growth, you then free yourself to update it when needed.

The purpose of the morning routine is to take control of, and build momentum into, your day. That's it. Cute phrases like "win the morning, win the day" have some truth to them. If you use the morning routine to build momentum and then use that momentum to get important work done, you've certainly won. But the routine itself didn't cause the win; it only set the conditions for it.

Expecting a morning routine to somehow magically make the rest of your life fall into place would be a huge mistake. That's like saying you'll be able to maintain good health if your breakfast is nutritious, but you eat junk food the rest of the day. So all you really need to do is use your morning routine to start the day in a strong, positive direction. That's not to suggest your morning routine isn't important. So when you get it nailed, give yourself a big pat on the back or a trophy, if that's what you always got growing up. Actually, don't give yourself a trophy just yet. You'll see that your morning routine is the foundation upon which you'll do so much more. When you consistently finish your most important work before 1:00 p.m., that's when you'll know you've accomplished something remarkable.

Now, to create a solid routine that works for you, use these five simple guidelines:

- Successful morning routines start the night before,
- Use activation energy when you wake, then
- Set your mind,
- Direct your self-talk, and
- Put your agenda first.

Success Starts the Night Before

A good night's sleep makes everything better the next day. I don't know anyone who doesn't believe that, yet I rarely hear sleep mentioned when people describe their morning routines. Nor do I know of a morning routine that can overcome a bad night's sleep. Sleep is for humans what plugging in to electricity is for a smartphone. So if you're really interested in waking up each day with the best possible charge for the day, you'll need to get serious about your sleep hygiene. Sleep hygiene is just a broad term used to describe your habits and environment regarding sleep.

These days, the hardest part of good sleep hygiene is putting down our glowy rectangles. Besides their addictive nature, unless you're using glasses that block 100 percent of the blue light coming from electronic devices, that blue light is going to hinder the production of the sleep-inducing hormone melatonin.

Imagine a stunning sunset radiating shades of yellow, orange, and red. As the sun sets each evening, the wavelength of the light we see lengthens toward the yellow and red end of the spectrum. This signals to our bodies it's time to produce more melatonin and prepare to sleep. When you block that natural process, it compromises sleep. That means staring at a screen late into the evening, even under the pretense of squeezing in extra work, backfires on you the next day. Between excessive blue light and constant screen time, you're messing with two hormones: melatonin and dopamine.

I've heard podcasts where people have become a bit manic with their sleep routines. They've gone to the extreme by making sure their rooms are so dark they can't even see their hand in front of their face. They've obsessed about the exact room and mattress temperatures.

One popular podcaster advocates the installation of a Faraday cage around your bed to block out all wireless signals and dirty electricity. He even promotes a grounding mattress to mimic sleeping on the actual ground.

If all that is exciting to you, I say go for it. Geek out to your heart's content. But for most people, a good night's sleep comes down to a few basic practices:

- Make your room dark and cool—68 degrees seems by consensus the ideal.
- Get off your devices at least an hour before bed; two hours would be better.
- Keep your sleep times reasonably consistent, even on weekends. I'm in bed by 9:00 each evening and up at

5:00 each day. On weekends, I shift to 10:00 p.m. and 6:00 a.m. and rarely vary from that.

- Eat your last meal two hours before bedtime. Your body can't digest food and prepare to sleep at the same time.
- Limit coffee after noon. Coffee in the afternoon never seems to bother me personally, but I still avoid it because I don't use a sleep tracker like the Oura Ring and can't be totally sure caffeine isn't having some effect on my sleep.
- Eliminating alcohol is also a no-brainer when your goal is to optimize sleep. That glass of wine might relax you at first but will wake you up right when you should be entering deep sleep because your body is processing the sugar.
- When it comes to your bed, make it off limits to everything except sleep, sex, and sickness/recovery. That way, your body knows what's going to happen when you get in it. You'll be sleeping, healing, or, well, you know. You should ban glowy rectangles of all kinds, including TVs, from your bedroom.

One other habit that can impede restful sleep is worrying about what is coming up the next day. Some people find it incredibly hard to relax in the evening and get their mind off what's coming up, especially if they perceive those events as stressful. So in chapter 6, I'll talk about how to keep work from creeping into your home life each evening.

Use Activation Energy

Let's assume you've got your sleep hygiene in order. When the alarm goes off, if you're not feeling it, hit the snooze button, right? NO WAY! Just forget about the existence of the snooze button. We go to bed never knowing if we're going to wake up for goodness' sake. Why would we ever want to go back to sleep?

Okay, so I'm teasing you a little to make a point. There are definitely times where it's fine to wake up and snooze or ease yourself out of bed and into the day. I'm thinking about weekends, vacations, and holidays. But on a normal weekday, the snooze button does the exact opposite of what we need, which is to build momentum.

In chemistry, activation energy is the minimum amount of energy required to trigger a reaction between two chemicals. For example, pushing the start button (or turning the key) in your car creates a spark of energy that activates the burning of gasoline in the engine. Without the energy of that spark, the gas sits there doing nothing. Likewise, you need a spark when you wake up.

Some people wake up and immediately put on their workout clothes and head to the gym. Some jump in a cold shower first. Others may start coffee and eat breakfast or walk the dog. Anything that works for you, other than hitting the snooze button, will do. Whatever you do, throwing the covers off and getting out of bed as fast as possible is the key.

What do you need to do to activate your energy and ensure you hop out of bed with enthusiasm?

Set Your Mind

A big part of an effective morning routine is setting your mind for the day. When you wake up, do you have a habit of deliberately cultivating a positive mindset, or do you end up with a mind that is set for you based on what you see and hear throughout the morning? Most people do the latter because they think of mindset as something that they have as opposed to something they create.

Mindset is most commonly used as a noun, but I find it helpful to break the word up and turn it into a phrase with an action verb. To cultivate a positive mindset, you have to "set your mind." When we sleep, our minds can take us on a variety of rides. We have dreams that make no sense, dreams that we forget ten seconds after opening our eyes, dreams that scare us into a waking scream, dreams that inspire us—and sometimes we recall nothing at all.

No one knows for certain what's going on up there other than to say our brains are using our subconscious minds to sort out tons of information each night. But when you wake up with a full charge and take over with your conscious mind, you have the ability to set your mind in any direction you wish it to go.

In my experience, when people describe their morning routines, it feels a lot like they're mimicking someone else's routine. Someone they admired talked about what they did on a podcast, so they implement it into their own life. Instead of doing that, think about the specifics of the morning routine as deliberately chosen activities that set the mind. Instead of blindly copying someone else, choose for yourself.

For example, you could consider meditation, yoga, uplifting music, positive affirmations, journaling, reading scripture, or a morning walk. There are no right or universally applicable activities for setting your mind in a positive direction. It only matters that what you do creates positive emotions for you.

At the end of this chapter, I describe my morning routine, but only as an example to help become more intentional. If you don't enjoy writing, journaling may not be your thing. If you're an atheist like my dad was, reading the Bible won't cut it. I have a friend who falls asleep when he reads, so that's the last activity he'll want to include in a morning routine.

Direct Your Self-Talk (Don't Use Words Against Yourself)

To fully experience the benefits of an effective morning routine, you'll have to actively direct your self-talk. This practice will help you maintain and build upon how you set your mind.

Let's say your morning routine includes a bit of meditation and expressing gratitude in your journal. If the next thing you do is go to the gym and start beating yourself up for carrying more body fat than you want, you've started to undo the work you put into meditation and journaling. And many of us have a bad habit of using words against ourselves.

Think about it. When you finished your last cheat meal, did the way you treat yourself make you feel guilty? Have you ever worked on a project at work while suffering from those nasty thoughts of unworthiness we label as impostor syndrome? When you scrolled through social media recently, was there a part of you that said you'd never be as pretty or as fit as the people you saw? Do you see what I mean?

The truth is that you can either let others influence your inner dialogue or you can take ownership of it. This is where affirmations can be of service. Most people think of affirmations as a positive statement, but affirmations can be positive or negative. *To affirm* is a verb and you can affirm something that feels good or bad. If you're in the gym constantly beating yourself up because you think you're fat, all you're doing is affirming (giving more energy to) the weight you'd like to drop. Conversely, if you say to yourself, "every workout brings me closer to my ideal figure," you're affirming your progress toward improved health.

One day I was riding in a car with a friend, and he was playing a podcast of a speaker discussing the law of attraction. The speaker said, "You get what you think about whether you want it or not." That statement instantly resonated as true in my gut and forever changed how I approached this topic. The lesson points to why positive affirmations are helpful for directing your self-talk. They help you think about what you want versus what you don't. If you accept the basic premise of that speaker's statement, you become empowered to more frequently choose to dwell on thoughts that will lead to your desired outcome. Often, this gets to the heart of building confidence.

Most of us would never talk to our loved ones like we talk to ourselves. Would you chastise your daughter for being fat or your spouse for being inferior to their peers? Of course not, but who hasn't been guilty of doing something similar to themselves? If you wouldn't talk like that to someone you care about, then you must not use words against yourself.

When I was nineteen and in my first sales training course, my instructor gave me an assignment. The assignment was to write out a series of affirmations, read them into a tape recorder (remember this was in the early 1990s), and play the recording every day as I drove to the office. That way, as I heard my voice speaking positive affirmations, I'd be conditioning my self-talk for the day.

I wrote out statements like, "I am the company top producer" and "I effortlessly earn $10,000 a month"—neither of which was true at the time. My recording was about three minutes long, and I was so far away from the life I affirmed, this practice felt almost futile. But in those days, I was willing to do anything my coach said. So morning after morning, I'd play this recording on the drive to the office like a good student.

I don't remember when it happened, but before too long, I believed the story I was telling on that recording. I still wasn't living that life, but my attitude shifted when I heard my voice, often enough, speaking the life I desired into existence. By the end of the coaching program, I'd won the award for the most listings taken. I wasn't the overall company top producer yet, but I was on the way.

Eventually I was living the story on my personal affirmation recording, and over the years, I've kept it as a secret weapon, especially when I knew I was going to push myself far out of my comfort zone.

So, as you build out your morning routine, consider writing out your own personal affirmation statement and recording it into your smartphone. You'll feel silly at first just as I did (and, yes, your voice does sound like that), but when it comes to directing your self-talk, doesn't it sound better than literally anything else on your glowy rectangle?

Whether or not you add this assignment to your routine, let's make a deal: no using words against yourself, okay? That means you're agreeing not to think or speak criticisms or other negative words against yourself. There's a time for constructive criticism, but not when you're building momentum into your day.

If you'd like to listen to one of my own recordings, download it at *http://DoneBeforeOne.com/bonus*

Put Your Agenda First

An effective morning routine puts your agenda for the day first. This subtle but powerful shift will go a long way to curing your feelings of being overwhelmed—busy but not making measurable progress. Just as you decide how you spend your money, you must be willing to decide how you are going to spend your time, especially during the first half of the day.

Every email, text message, social media post, and phone call comes with another person's agenda. They're focused on what's important to the sender, which may or may not be what's important to you at the moment. You always have the choice to elevate other interests over your own and, sadly, many people do. Then they claim that constant interruptions prevent them from getting anything done. The harder truth to face is that most people allow themselves to be interrupted rather than develop the conviction and discipline to put themselves first.

If you're not used to putting yourself first, it'll help to get clear on the difference between reacting and responding. Reacting to an incoming stimulus is the right move if you're in danger. For example, if your kid throws a baseball and it's coming straight for your face, quickly reacting to get out of its path will save you from a bloody nose. If that same kid brought home a failing report card, instantly reacting by yelling at him wouldn't be the right move. As a good parent, you'd likely want to gather your thoughts first, then respond with a strategy to help. Likewise, you're typically not in some kind of immediate danger at work, so reacting is better saved for genuine emergencies.

Take a minute and think about the last few days. Have you been responding to people or reacting? If you're normal (and honest) you'll likely realize you've been reacting. It's so easy to get into a pattern of reacting. How many times do you refresh your inbox and then react to whatever appears? As you've been reading this book, how many times have you reacted to an incoming notification on your phone?

Reacting feels like important work, especially when you're reacting to a client. After all, replying to emails as fast as possible is excellent customer service, isn't it? Actually, not always. Granted, there are times when a situation is truly urgent and you need to drop what you're doing to take care of someone. But those times are few and far between, unless you're the one causing the chaos.

People who have a habit of reacting quickly to every incoming stimulus are often working hard to avoid doing the work they know is important, but are resisting. Salespeople and business owners of all kinds avoid prospecting, and writers avoid facing the blank page. You know you're putting your agenda first when you're willing to do those tasks critical to hitting your goals each day before you even consider anything else. Once the work you've discerned to be important is done, it's safe to respond to everything else.

To be sure, responding to situations is far more effective and professional than reacting. On some level, you know that staying focused is best for you and best for your client. When you stop reacting to everything around you, you'll begin to produce your best work. Why? Because reactions are instant, and a response requires space. While you're focused on your agenda, you're naturally creating space between you and everyone else.

We've all experienced times when we've been away from email for an extended period and the person who requested something from us at 9:00 a.m. sends another email at 11:45 a.m. letting us know they got it handled. They made a request, and because you were tied up, you didn't react. By the time you were able to choose between a reaction and a response, you didn't even need to.

If you truly commit to putting your agenda first each day, you'll see this play out. That so many others spend their day reacting plays to your advantage. While they're busy reacting to everything around them, you get to stay focused on your agenda, and when you're ready to respond, many of those people will have helped themselves.

My Routine

If I sold you on building your own morning routine using the principles I just covered, you don't really need to know mine. But I also know you want to know anyway, so here's what has worked for me, with only minor tweaks, for over a decade.

Before bed I lay out the "man of clothes" on the chair in my home office. This is what my dad taught me to do when I was little, probably to save himself time each morning, but it definitely saves me time as an adult. I lay out my gym clothes and outfit for the next day so I don't have to make those decisions the next morning.

I'm up at 5:00 a.m. and in bed by 9:00 p.m. on weekdays. On weekends and holidays, I wake up an hour later and rarely stay up past 10:00 p.m. Straying too far from those time frames negatively affects my energy, mood, and performance in pretty much everything.

When the alarm goes off, I jump out of bed and into a cold shower for roughly three minutes. This sounds awful, I know, and it was for the first couple of weeks, but now I'm addicted. When the cold water hits my skin, it triggers deep inhales of oxygen, which quickly wakes up my body and mind. Once I got used to the initial shock of the cold, it became an invigorating experience. By the way, if you try this, it's important to inhale through the nose to get the same effect.

Then I throw on my gym clothes, brush my teeth, and head out. This takes exactly twelve minutes. Remember activation energy? Springing out of bed and hitting the cold shower without thinking about it is how I use it in my routine. If you're scrutinizing the details and wondering, my partner, Jon, is on dog duty at this point.

After my workout, I grab coffee and take fifteen to thirty minutes to write in my daily planner, which is also my primary journal. I use the notes page for the day to dump out whatever is on my mind and how long this takes depends on what's swirling around in there. Usually that's a mix of what I'm grateful for, thoughts I had while working out, and whatever other random thoughts are bouncing around.

There are times when I'm feeling pressure or facing a challenge, and what ends up on the pages looks like a crazy person wrote it. Adversity or not, my mind is often racing fast in the morning, so getting whatever is in there out on the page helps me ground the energy and get focused. After all, the line between you and me and the person screaming as they walk down the street can be as thin as the page in the journal. Aren't you glad people can't hear all the thoughts going through your mind? I'm convinced journaling is one way to help keep us sane so we aren't the one walking down the sidewalk, letting our thoughts spill out of our mouths at high volume as everyone else avoids us. Anyway, next it's time to walk the pups and get showered and dressed for the day. I work from my home office and my goal each day is to be at my desk by 8:30 a.m. ready to tackle my top tasks for the day. Before I dive in, I'll do a quick scan of email and messages to see if there are any true emergencies. Hint: there are never any emergencies. One or two per year, that's it.

Then I review and begin working on the top three tasks for the day that I chose the day before. My mental battery is draining, so now it's a race to get tasks done before my brain hits power save mode.

More important than what I'm doing during my morning routine is what I'm not doing. I'm not listening to or reading news of any kind. I don't turn on the TV, and I don't listen to news radio shows. My drive to the gym is in silence. I don't hop on email and I don't open social media.

In the gym, I listen to dance music, and if I finish my journal/planner quickly, I'll read something motivational and inspiring. This is how I get into my day as my best self. It's how I bring my A game, for myself and for my clients.

But like I mentioned, nailing the morning routine is only part of the story. It builds positive momentum and sets you up for a successful day. Now let's work on getting some important shit done.

5

CONTROL THE FIRST HALF OF THE DAY

Remember, your agenda comes first, and that means you have to take responsibility for making the choice each day. How exactly are you going to spend your time?

Controlling the first half of the day is at the very core of the Done Before One lifestyle. The power of the concept comes from its simplicity: identify your most important tasks for the day, get them done before 1:00 p.m., and then get on with your life.

Nearly everyone I've introduced to the idea is immediately excited by it, but of course, the next thought they have is wondering how this plan could work for them.

Naturally, if you've been living a hectic life, that's driven by everyone's agenda but your own, it would seem impossible, or at the very least you'd be skeptical. That just makes you normal, but I have yet to work with anyone who wasn't able to realize this way of life for themselves. Yet simple doesn't always mean easy.

You've likely spent your entire life being conditioned into the opposite of a Done Before One life. Working hard, putting in long hours, sacrificing your personal life and even your health are values that are built into the Western world's narrative of what it means to be successful. I also value hard work and putting in long hours when needed. But I do not value long hours and hard work when they come at the expense of everything else in life, especially health.

Therefore, as you implement this method into your life, remember to go at your own speed. No one adopts practices like this exactly as they are taught anyway. As you work to break free of past conditioning, give yourself the grace to mess up and try again. Give yourself the time to see evidence of your work paying off as a more productive, enjoyable, and satisfying day. Eventually, you'll be stringing days into weeks and weeks into months.

Mindset Shift: Let's Work!

Now that you know how to design and use a morning routine that builds momentum and gets you primed to produce your best work, it's time to shift into work mode. Once you get to your place of work, wherever that is (even your spare bedroom), it would be a mistake to start randomly working to check items off your to-do list.

When I say it's time to shift into work mode, what I mean is it's time to tackle the truly important tasks in your business—the ones that trigger growth and build your business and bank accounts. These just happen to be the ones that push us out of our comfort zone and trigger enormous resistance. That's why less effective people than you dive into the easy tasks first. You've no doubt heard the phrase "eat the frog first" and that's essentially what I'm asking you to do. It requires a mindset shift and there are a couple of ways to make that happen.

One of the best practices is to make sure you dress for success. Just because you can run around in athleisure all day doesn't mean you should. When I first started in business at eighteen, I instinctively wore a tie to the office. As you know, in those days, I was a real estate agent, and no one dreamed of going into the office in workout gear. In fact, the office had a dress code so you literally couldn't dress down.

Ties were an inexpensive way for me to meet the office requirement but also very hot for most of the year in Austin, Texas, so as my income grew, I upgraded to breathable wool trousers and unstructured sport coats. Initially, I was just trying not to get hassled by the office manager, but eventually the sport coat and pocket square became a mindset shifting uniform for me. When the sport coat was on, it meant I was in work mode, both physically and mentally. I'm sure this is the same feeling a doctor gets when putting on the white coat.

I still love neckties, but to this day, sport coats and pocket squares are my thing. As I'm writing this, I'm sitting in my home office alone dressed for success. Not because I have to, but because I care enough about the work to make sure I'm in the right mindset. Along the way, I had a client teach me about Swiss mechanical watches, so now in addition to the sport coat, the wristwatch I'm wearing adds additional meaning and energy to the work I'm doing each day.

When my mentors taught me to dress for success, they were helping me shift into a new mindset, one that would prepare me to produce. It's a way of showing respect for yourself and for your client or customer. A sport coat and nice watch may not be ideal for your profession, especially if you're a personal trainer. In that case, a nice polo with your logo embroidered on the chest will put you into a productive mindset.

What physical symbol will you use?

The Job vs. the Reward

Another way to get into the right mindset is to understand your job. Your actual job is not what you may have thought it was before we met in this book. When you're an entrepreneur or self-employed in any capacity, your primary job, in fact your only job, is to generate leads, schedule appointments, and make sales. Everything you thought was the job (and that your competition still does) is actually the reward.

If you understand this correctly, you are less likely to give up and get a real job.

To be clear, your business is definitely real, so don't get offended. When I say real job, I mean the 9-to-5 steady paycheck W-2 type employment that makes you sick to your stomach to even think about. So listen, this isn't a book on marketing and salesmanship, but as you know, those are also my areas of expertise. The last thing you need is loved ones making statements like, "Shouldn't you think about getting a real job?" because they're nervous you aren't making enough money.

I don't know how the term *'real job'* got into our collective consciousness. I only know that, over the years, my clients who have been struggling for a while all reported having to resist the pressure from home to think about getting one. I also know no one wants to hear it. When you implement a Done Before One lifestyle, chances plummet you'll ever hear those words.

If you've never thought about it this way, it's definitely a mindset shift. When I worked with new real estate agents, they always thought their job was to sell the house. Agents focus most of their daily activities on selling the listing or finding a house for the buyer. The best agents, however, understood that they only got the privilege of working with a seller or a buyer because prior to that, they did their real job—generate the lead.

It's the same no matter what industry you want to pick. Personal trainers think their job is to help people with their workouts, but that's just the reward. No leads means no clients, which means no workouts. One of my past clients from my days as a Realtor called me after I'd moved into coaching because she'd left a huge law firm in order to open her own practice. She is a litigator and a good one, but she wanted more direct control over her clients than she was getting while working for a massive firm.

The first thing I helped her do was shift her mindset so she was absolutely clear on one thing: no leads means no clients, which means she wouldn't be suing anyone, which meant she'd never be in the courtroom doing what she truly loved. It clicked with her instantly. She loved being in the courtroom so much it felt like a reward to her. She was already good at the reward side of the equation. Our work together was focused on getting her good at the job.

Let's face it, if you have no business, then who cares if you're done before 1:00 p.m.? You have to be sold on identifying and diving into your most important work first, each day. The way you know you're sold is when you do your "real job" with enthusiasm. It's even baked into the word: the last four letters of enthusIASM stand for I Am Sold Myself.

When it becomes unacceptable for you to do anything else in your day before you've worked on the activities that drive your income, you'll want to make sure you have a smart tax accountant and investment adviser to help you handle all of your cash.

So you're at work, dressed for success, you look the part and understand the true job and are enthusiastic about the reward. Now the rubber meets the road. It's time to start "working," but where do you start? The answer: start with your top three tasks.

The Daily Top Three

Living a Done Before One lifestyle requires mastery over the concept of the daily top three. The better you are at identifying your top three most important tasks for the day, the better your life will be overall.

I was lucky that early on I had a mentor who made certain I understood how important it was to develop the skill of deciding what my top three would be each day. All self-employed people face a long list of tasks they could do on a given day, but it wasn't until I started coaching that I learned many people struggle to pick three from their list.

Eventually, I learned most people were thinking about their to-do list in its entirety. That would stress me out, too, and I can see how it easily leads to paralysis by analysis. The way to keep from being overwhelmed is to think of your work in three ways: goals, projects, and tasks. Broadly speaking, you have goals and to achieve those goals, you'll need to complete projects. Of course, you don't do a project all at once. You have individual tasks that add up to project completion.

Once you've decided which projects need to be completed to accomplish your goals, it will become clear which specific task comes next with each project. These specific tasks determine your next actions, and your daily top three tasks are derived from your next actions.

Clearly, lead generation must be one of them if you sell your products and services yourself. At a higher level, it might be to mentor and train your salespeople. Beyond lead generation, the tasks you choose as your top three each day should have two basic outcomes:

- Nudge you toward your quarterly goals and
- Stay as close as possible to the money

Remember, for each of the projects you have to support your goals, there are corresponding next actions that need to be completed. The more clarity you have around your goals, the easier it will be to identify projects and next actions and then pick your top three items for the day. I'll talk more about goals in chapter 7, but for now, it's less important to be crystal clear on every goal than it is to internalize the power of choosing your top three action items each day.

Remember, your agenda comes first, and that means you have to take responsibility for making the choice each day. How exactly are you going to spend your time? Whenever I'm working with someone who's having trouble landing on a decision, I ask them this question:

- "If your workday stopped at 1:00 p.m. today and you literally couldn't do anything after that time, what are the three most important action items you must get done?"

That question typically focuses the mind enough to make the right decisions, but if you're still having trouble, think about where you are most uncomfortable. What is on your to-do list that you resist the most? Those items almost always belong in your top three.

Sometimes, three can be one. I mean, there are going to be days when if you just got one huge, very important task done, and that's it, you'll have accomplished a ton. So while most days you'll be sacrificing items on your list in favor of the most important three, there are going to be times when you narrow your focus to just one or two big tasks.

The goal is the feeling of accomplishment and satisfaction that comes from putting in a good day's work. Not a hectic day of people-pleasing switching between the stuff everyone else wants from you, but an honest day of tackling the stuff you know you need to do to succeed.

You see, most people I've worked with initially do the opposite. Most people I've worked with initially do the opposite by filling the first part of their day with busy work - easy tasks that give them the feeling of being productive as they assure themselves they'll get to the harder parts in the afternoon. They say, first let me take care of these other people, then I'll take care of myself. Of course, the hard stuff rarely gets done in the afternoon, and by the time they get home, they're beating themselves up because they have accomplished nothing that gets them closer to their goals.

Eventually, deadlines force the real work to get done, and sometimes the deadline is tied to the bank account. When a person is in danger of not being able to pay their bills on time, they become really good at muscling through all the tasks they were resisting in order to get some money coming in. But once the deadline passes, once the bank account has some money in it again and the pressure is off, the old pattern of avoidance reemerges.

This is a stressful way to move through your career. By now, you should sense that you don't have to. Even if you're brand new and aren't totally sure what your projects and next actions should be (like me at the beginning of my career), you can start by randomly picking three items and committing to them. Give yourself the chance to see what it feels like to make the choice and follow through. That, in and of itself, is success. From there, you can practice each day making better (and braver) choices.

Block Your Time: How to Use Your Calendar

I've been mentioning a thing called the "to-do list" but the truth is, successful people don't work from a traditional to-do list. A to-do list offers little to no help because it ignores the time component of the task. Instead, they work from their calendar using time blocking. Time blocking is simply using your calendar to block out the time required to do the tasks you've agreed to do.

Some people take time blocking way too far because they equate being busy with success and with being a good leader or an important person in their industry. In an attempt to be seen that way, they will unconsciously jam-pack their calendar and then broadcast their "busyness" to anyone who will listen. But what they are really broadcasting is that they never say no and have no boundaries. A full calendar in this context just means the person says yes to everything, is a people pleaser, and, worse, ineffective at their job. In other words, the opposite of how they wish to be seen.

On the flip side, there are those who resist time blocking because to them it feels restrictive. Especially to the self-employed person who may have left corporate America in part to get out of their overly scheduled, meeting-driven life. The last thing they want to hear about is time blocking. They have a strong desire to control their own time, but miss the fact that *control* is a verb. So in an act of rebellion against their old life, they control nothing, say yes to too many requests, and end up over-committed just as before. Only now it's worse because they have no calendar to reference!

Neither approach is effective or sustainable. Observing people struggle with both extremes provided a lot of inspiration for formalizing the Done Before One method. Early on, when I was coaching people, I needed a way to convince them to use their calendar in a thoughtful way. I brought the two extremes to the middle by helping them internalize the following three concepts.

1. **Translate Everything into an Appointment**

First, I taught them to think of everything as an appointment. Not just a formal business meeting, but everything they did in their day. Need to put your head down and write a report?

That's an appointment. Need time to clear your email inbox? That's also an appointment. Going to the gym? That's another appointment. Grocery store later? Appointment. Shopping for a new outfit? Yep, that's an appointment. Getting your hair cut? You got it. Appointment.

By the way, there's no law that says appointments must have other people present. You can have an appointment with yourself, and as you think this way, you become highly aware of how much time you need to spend for each activity. It's also a sobering experience because you quickly see how much time you *don't* have to do all the unnecessary activities you have a habit of trying to squeeze in. This is the beginning of undoing a busy life.

Some of you are going to have to trust me when I say there is freedom in an appropriate amount of structure. I understand the idea of making every task an appointment will feel like I'm putting chains on you at first, but it's this self-imposed structure that creates the freedom people are after.

Picture yourself identifying your top three tasks for the day, then translating them to a block of time on your calendar, ideally before 1:00 p.m. When those tasks are done, or said better, when those appointments are complete, you can pat yourself on the back because you'll have outproduced everyone around you. What happens in the afternoon won't matter much.

If you've ever had a productive morning followed by an afternoon where you lost all control, you know you still feel pretty good about yourself in the evening. But if you've ever failed to control the morning and get critical work done and then your afternoon fell apart, you likely know the feeling of beating yourself up over what you didn't get done. Seriously, if you attend those morning appointments successfully, let your afternoon fall apart. Schedule nothing, fly by the seat of your pants, be unfocused and scatterbrained if you want. You'll still have outproduced your peers. The more mornings like that you string together, the more unstoppable you'll become.

2. Stop When the Appointment Ends

Second, I coach people about the importance of stopping when the time block ends. This is obvious when you are attending a well-run meeting. If the meeting is scheduled for an hour and has a strong leader, once sixty minutes pass, the meeting ends and everyone moves on. When you're attending an appointment with yourself, it's important to maintain that same level of discipline.

For example, if one of your top three tasks for the day is to make follow-up calls for one hour, stay present and focused for that sixty minutes, and when time is up, allow yourself to move on. If you scheduled thirty minutes to return messages, allow yourself to move on when a half hour has passed.

We don't live in the *Star Trek* era where we can transport ourselves instantly across space. It takes time to transition from one thing to another, especially if you intend to be focused and present for the next task. If you don't want to be that person who's seven minutes late for everything, then stopping what you're doing at the end of each time block will become necessary.

In my experience, people who have a problem with this are those who aren't even aware of how they are spending their time. The fact that you're reading this makes you different. At the very least, you have an interest in improving the flow of your day. So one day at a time, as you work on time blocking your tasks, practice stopping on time and allowing transition time.

3. Leave White Space

The third concept in time blocking is to leave white space. You simply cannot block out every second of the day and be effective. In fact, it'll just leave you exhausted and depressed. Think of blocking time the same way you think of spending money. You don't spend money mindlessly all day, do you? Certainly, you pull back at times and think about how you want to spend your hard-earned cash.

Successful people have that same attitude when it comes to spending their time. White space or open, unscheduled time on the calendar is time to think about your work, your life, and what really matters. Even Marcus Aurelius struggled with this. One translation in his book *Meditations* has the line, "Is this essential? Is this really what I'm trading my life for?" When you spend money, you're trading it for goods and services. When you spend time, you're trading it for your life.

Thinking about every task as an appointment doesn't mean you should schedule every second of the day. Consider the time necessary to do what you intend to do, block sufficient time on your calendar, move on when time is up, and leave open space in the day for the unexpected.

Advanced Tricks

The Done Before One lifestyle is easy to understand and to live. It's also easy to get off track. Here are some advanced tricks you can use to keep from sabotaging yourself.

- **Stop interrupting yourself.** At some point, you have to take responsibility for your actions. If your phone rings and you're busy but still answer it, don't fool yourself into thinking the caller interrupted you. The truth is that YOU interrupted yourself when you decided to break your focus and answer the phone. If you haven't turned off notifications on your mobile phone, blaming the phone or social media doesn't help. You have ultimate control over your glowy rectangles, so turn them off when you need to focus.

- **Manage outside interruptions—that is, other people.** When it comes to in-person interruptions, a physical object signaling you aren't interruptible works wonders. In the past I've used a sign that displays the number 1,440 in a huge font size. In that office setting, I let everyone know when that sign was visible, I needed to focus. I made sure they understood there were only 1,440 minutes in a day, and if they saw the sign, they were not to interrupt me to ask for any of them.

  You can use any object that has meaning for you. In my experience, that 8.5 x 11 framed sign acted like a force field once people around me understood its meaning and realized I was serious. I'd even see people look away and reroute their path if they were walking toward me and caught a glimpse of that sign.

  If you work from home and are prone to interruption from other household members, try closing the door to your office and hanging the sign from the doorknob or just tape it up at eye level. I suppose a simple "Do Not Disturb" door hangar could work as well, but it doesn't have the flair or drama of an image that highlights the value of time for all who see it. If you don't want to spend any of your minutes creating the sign, I've done it for you. You can download it in the bonus section at *www.donebeforeone.com/bonus*

- **Mindfully shift tasks.** Rather than moving from one task to another as fast as humanly possible, when you finish one thing, stop and give yourself three minutes to focus on what's next. Often I'll close my eyes and breathe deeply while considering what I'm about to do and visualize the ideal outcome. For example, before switching into a coaching call, I'll often visualize myself speaking to my client and imagining them experiencing emotions like relief, enthusiasm, and happiness at the end of our session.

- **Use your calendar as your defender.** The next four words can change your life if you let them: "Can't then. I'm booked." You don't have control over how many times you get asked to do something, but you have control over your response. People who have a chronic problem over-committing could use this advice the most. Every week, I watch people spend huge amounts of time rearranging their calendar. It never fails. You design your perfect morning and block it out on your calendar only to have someone come along and ask to meet with you at the same time. It's like life is testing you to see if you are serious. The average person will compromise, change their schedule, and justify it as good customer service. What they don't realize is the damage this does to their self-confidence.

    When you tell yourself you're going to do something and further solidify it by blocking out the time on your calendar, only to change it later based on an outside request, you break trust with yourself. This is subtle but real nonetheless, and can cause intensely negative self-talk.

    Everyone would agree it's important to keep your commitments to others, but few consider the importance of keeping commitments to yourself. Confidence comes from taking action and being impeccable with your word, to quote from the book *The Four Agreements*, especially when those words are in the form of self-talk. But the great thing about the solution is that you don't have to say no or otherwise create drama around something that can be straightforward and simple.

When someone wants you to spend your time on their agenda and you've already blocked it out for your agenda, just say, "Can't then, I'm booked." As long as you stop with those four words and don't try to justify or explain what's already on your calendar, people will simply pick another time. Never in my life have I told someone I'm booked and have them say, "Oh yeah? Booked doing what?" That just doesn't happen because people aren't that confrontational. They'll just assume what you have booked is important. And it should be, or else why would you be planning to spend the time in the first place?

- **Renegotiate agreements when needed.** For the overwhelming majority of the time, you should have no problem holding your time blocks in the morning, but sometimes you'll have an urgent issue arise that needs to be dealt with, and doing so will require you to adjust your schedule. What I'm talking about here are true emergencies where your presence or input is critical.

  Before you drop everything and jump into the deep end, take a minute and renegotiate your agreement with yourself. You said you were going to do X and now you are choosing to break that agreement; be honest with yourself about why you are going to do that. Acknowledge the benefit of breaking the agreement and the cost of the change. Then reschedule that broken agreement in a new time block and recommit.

Be very cautious here. We all like to think of ourselves as indispensable when it comes to our work, but that's ego talking. True emergencies where your input is critical are exceedingly rare. As you read in my morning routine, every morning when I'm transitioning into work mode, I do a quick scan of email, text, and direct messages to see if there is anything both urgent and important. If you really pressed me, I'd have a hard time identifying three times a year when something truly important came up.

That doesn't mean I'm not tempted to jump into situations where I can help. If I have a challenging task ahead of me or if my mindset is simply not as focused on any given day, it would be easy to start responding and use incoming messages as an excuse to avoid the more important work I'd planned to do. Salespeople and business owners do this all the time. They have prospecting on their calendar and then read an urgent message from a current client, confuse it as important, and use the situation as an excuse to drop prospecting like a hot potato.

The key here is to be honest with yourself about the difference between what's urgent and important. From others' point of view, every incoming message is urgent. You have to learn to discern for yourself if it's also important enough to drop everything and lose control of the most important part of your day. If it truly is, renegotiate your time blocks and let yourself off the hook. If you find yourself doing this frequently, consider it a red flag.

- **No explanation is necessary.** Resisting the temptation to explain yourself, which tends to come from some deep-seated guilt, is difficult for many people. I once had a client who blamed her Catholic upbringing for her persistent feelings of guilt, especially when it came to controlling how she spent her own time.

To help people in this situation, I've often taught them another four-letter phrase: "Love to, can't now." This is similar to telling people you're booked but carries a distinct energy. Sometimes people aren't asking for a specific time on your calendar, but they interrupt you anyway. If guilt consciousness plagues you, the phrase "love to, can't now" can make a big difference.

Picture this: You're at your desk clearly focused and an inconsiderate coworker prances up and asks if you have a minute. Some people can simply shoot the coworker a look that says, "Scram, idiot, can't you see I'm focused?" Others will have no problem saying it out loud, but most of us need something softer. When you say, "Love to, can't now," you soften the blow a little and imply that you're willing to help at another time. The trick is not explaining yourself. Why you can't help them at this very moment is none of their business. How you spend your time requires no more explanation to others than how you spend your money.

- **Stop over-promising**. A mentor once asked me what the goal of good customer service was. After a few typical answers like "to take care of the client" and "to make the client happy," he stopped me and said, "No. You get no brownie points for taking care of your clients. You're supposed to do that. The goal of customer service is to go beyond the basics of taking care of customers and show up as a pleasant surprise. If they feel like interactions with you are a pleasant surprise, they'll be happy, they'll come back, and they'll send you referrals often."

He was spot on and over time, I learned the best way to show up as a pleasant surprise was to simply do what I said I'd do. People who over-promise have the best of intentions but sadly end up under-delivering most of the time. Think about how many times recently someone has under-delivered service to you. How far back do you have to go before you identify an instance where someone lost control of their day and changed an appointment with you? When was the last time someone promised to send you something, like a report or resource for a project, only to never mention it again?

Again, people have good intentions but because they aren't in the habit of connecting tasks with time and using their calendar, they chronically under-deliver. None of this is catastrophic, but it gives you an enormous opportunity to stand out in a positive way. If you're careful and deliberate about what you say you'll do, and remember to think about the time required before you open your mouth, you'll rarely over-promise. And because literally everyone else does, you become a pleasant surprise, which is to say, you become seen as a highly dependable person. If occasionally you find time to go beyond what you said you'd do, even better. Do what you say you'll do, sometimes more, never less.

- **Break the email and wait culture.** Modern business can feel like a bunch of people firing off emails and waiting for a response. It's sort of hilarious when you picture people sending dozens of emails a day, each waiting for the other to reply. This is a problem because, if you need to get your most important work Done Before One, you won't always have time to wait for a response.

When I'm coaching people, they sometimes tell me they are stuck because so-and-so hasn't gotten back to them. When I ask what they've done about it, I'm usually told they sent another email. Any more than that and they feel they are being pushy. For someone trained from the beginning as a salesperson, I find this nuts. Being pushy is an obnoxious personality trait. We all know someone like that and I don't advocate for it. But being professionally persistent is something different altogether.

Just as you could name a pushy person, I'm certain you can also name someone who has a reputation for getting shit done. These people are looked up to partly because they don't send emails and wait. If they need a faster response, they might follow up with a text or a phone call to nudge the task along. In other words, they vary their approach until the other person responds, all the while being professional in their communication.

If you want to maximize your Done Before One lifestyle, you'll need to practice being professionally persistent. That means learning to stop emailing people when you should call them. In a perfect world, every working person would buy and read this book, but since that's not going to happen, you can bet the odds are in your favor that people will interrupt themselves to help you. Sucks for them, but great for you. If these people are on your team, get what you need first, then give them a copy of this book.

- **Let the afternoon fall apart.** I've mentioned this before and it's important enough to restate several times. If you are intent on controlling the first half of the day, allow the afternoon to descend into chaos if it must. This is essential for more controlling personalities, like myself. As much as we may want to control everything around us all day, life often has other plans.

Controlling what happens in the morning fulfills that need and allows us to be productive. Leaving the afternoon unstructured opens up space for life to happen. If your friend wants to go to a late lunch and have a few drinks and you've controlled the morning, you'll be able to go and enjoy the afternoon guilt-free provided your schedule is open. But if you've been unfocused all morning, you'll face a no-win situation: say yes to your friend and beat yourself up later because you got nothing done or say no to your friend and disappoint them.

- **Building a habit is the most important task.** When I was new in business, I observed successful people living their own Done Before One lifestyle long before I named it as such. When I started to mimic their behavior, I didn't understand yet what my most important tasks were. But I did sense the importance of the pattern and happened to be surrounded by great mentors. Instinctively, I did my best to focus on the pattern and trusted my mentors would help me figure out the specifics. That's exactly what happened.

  As you are working on designing and implementing these concepts, if you don't know exactly what to do in the morning, know this: establishing the pattern is most important. You can find coaches and mentors from your specific industry who can help you fill in the details. But remember, your first aim is to establish and hold the pattern.

- **Don't say "My brain doesn't work that way."** Yes, it does and you're only fooling yourself if you think otherwise. I've had clients resist the Done Before One lifestyle because they failed to understand the freedom it brings. While I understand imposing this kind of structure on yourself feels restrictive at first, the most successful people in all industries, including the creatives and artists, eventually learn the structure provides the freedom.

When someone says their brain doesn't work that way, what they're really saying is that they haven't learned to manage their emotions. Being focused and getting truly important work done during the first half of the day automatically puts you in the zone of growth. All growth is uncomfortable, so rather than telling yourself that your brain doesn't work that way, at least be honest and say, "I haven't learned to control my emotions when growth makes me uncomfortable." A better approach would be to affirm: I am comfortable being uncomfortable because it's a sign my life is improving.

Now you have almost everything you need to design your own Done Before One lifestyle. You know how to build momentum into your day using an effective morning routine. You know how to shift your mind into productivity mode, and you know how to establish and work through your daily top three. Of course, some days you'll be done by exactly 1:00 p.m.; other days it might be 10:30 a.m.; and still other days it may be 2:00 p.m. before you've finished your top three.

Remember, 1:00 p.m. is a guideline, not a hard rule. Each day, you can pick your target time to be done with your important tasks, with the goal of being as close to midday as possible. Done Before One is also a mindset, an attitude, and an inspirational mantra. It's a rallying cry to reclaim your time and use work to generate the funds to actually go live a full life. In any case, you're done, so how do you set yourself up for the next day? That's the next chapter.

6

HOW TO LET GO OF WORK EACH DAY

The Done Before One lifestyle, when executed fully as intended, forms an energetic loop that takes all the momentum and progress generated in a day and feeds it into the next day.

ne of the most important keys to living a Done Before One lifestyle successfully is finishing your day strong.

I used to think that only self-employed people had trouble putting work away, but eventually I realized that hardly anyone these days finishes the day in a way that sets them up for success the next day. In fact, the more mobile technology has invaded our lives, the less likely we are to ever finish a workday—strong, weak, or otherwise. Work follows us around wherever we go, and unfortunately, it can feel like dragging around an anchor. You may be strong enough to drag an anchor behind you, but do you really want to?

There was a time we could go into the world undistracted and live life without being constantly on call. I'm dating myself here, but back then it was sufficient to check messages on the answering machine when we got home or to check voice mail when we got back to our desk. I'm not suggesting we should go backward, but the downside of today's mobile technology is that if we don't have the discipline to use technology in a way that serves us, we'll simply serve it.

When technology isn't serving you, your work and everyone else's agenda will forever drag behind you, never too heavy at any one moment but constantly wearing you down until finally you're ready to do something about it. I trust if you've read to this point, you're ready to cut the rope and drop the anchor.

I knew I was at that drop-the-anchor moment even before the age of the smartphone. I'd built my real estate practice to a point where my phone never stopped ringing. Do you remember the Motorola RAZR flip phone? It didn't need a case, and you could throw it across your desk (or the room if it was that kind of day) and not worry about breaking it. I kept my phone on vibrate mode and one day watched as it vibrated itself off my desk and fell against the wall. I left it there until it vibrated itself to a dead battery.

At that time, I had become really good at getting my most productive work (lead generation) Done Before One, which is why my phone was ringing off the hook with leads and clients. I was grateful to be in demand, but had to learn how to tame the monster I'd created.

In the evenings and on weekends, I was jealous of my W-2 employed friends who seemed to so easily put work out of their minds when they left the office. Little did I know at the time they were no better off. So here I was holding on to two competing mindsets: one where I was grateful for my business and the other resenting it. One of those mindsets had to win, and I knew which one.

That's when I decided I needed to design a way to finish the day that was just as powerful as the way I'd started it in order to regain some peace. I needed to learn to finish the day deliberately and with intention.

When designing the end of the day, the goal is to create a powerful loop that feeds the momentum of the current day into the next. It's not complicated, but it takes some practice and a few clever tricks. Here's how you do it.

When Does Work Stop for the Day?

I was almost convinced that the pandemic finally shattered our long-standing attitude that the workday ends at 5:00 p.m.

After all, at the time I'm writing this (summer 2023) I can pull up a long list of stories about the death of commercial real estate. Office towers in cities all over the country have soaring vacancy rates, and corporations are working hard in the face of intense resistance to convince their employees to come back to the office. So I thought, okay, times are changing. Then I checked out rush hour.

I had to check it out because one of the hidden benefits of a Done Before One lifestyle is that you won't have to get out into rush hour traffic. You're able to design your day away from it. But many people clearly still commute because morning and evening rush hour are just as bad as they've ever been. I checked this out personally in Los Angeles and in other cities such as Austin, Dallas, and Phoenix by asking my real estate agent friends who must constantly know traffic patterns so they don't waste huge amounts of time sitting in their car.

I learned that although more people than ever are working from home, their mindset is still stuck in a 9-to-5 pattern.

The Done Before One lifestyle shatters that Industrial Age concept. I don't care what hours you work, as long as you decide for yourself instead of getting trapped in the herd.

When you choose to stop work each day is separate from when you finish your top three tasks. If you're done with your most important work by exactly 1:00 p.m. and want to stop work, great. If you finish at 2:45 p.m. and choose to keep going, okay. No day will be exactly the same, so the key is to ask yourself a question: When does work stop today?

When I ask this of others, I often get a confused look. I can tell it's something few have ever considered, at least not since the last time they had a job, like fast-food, where they clocked out at the end of their shift. The question itself is powerful because it prompts you to make a decision to put work away and live the rest of your life. And when you think about it, you have always made a choice. Not consciously deciding to put work away each day is a choice.

As easy as it is to pick a time to stop working, it can certainly be anxiety-inducing. What if you miss an important client call? What if you miss a prospect and lose out on a sale? "But, Jasen, I need to be available to show I'm committed. If I don't respond right away, it's poor customer service."

These are all normal thoughts. So are deeper and darker thoughts like these: "I've worked so much, I'm embarrassed I'm out of touch with my kids." "I've worked so much, intimacy is gone in my relationship." "I've worked so much, my friends never invite me to anything anymore." The avoidance of these damaged areas of your life will also keep you from putting work away.

So listen, first you must know that no one enjoys working with stressed-out people who never give themselves a break. Would you rather be operated on by a surgeon who is available 24/7 because, you know, "good customer service," or by a surgeon who just got back from a relaxing vacation and is ready to get back to work?

Second, you must know you are much more than one deal or customer. You can't work every lead or serve every customer in your industry. You don't need to and you shouldn't want to. If you're sensing this fear of loss could be a challenge for you, it's a sign of scarcity thinking. There are 8 billion people on the planet, and you must believe enough of them are eager for you to find them and offer your product or service. This means one deal, one customer more or less, won't break you. But the inability to honor other parts of your life will get you in the long term.

Third, if you are working because it's an easy way to avoid facing other parts of your life, you should know that you can't run forever. Those uncomfortable areas of life you are avoiding will only get worse the longer you ignore them. Life can be terrifying. I absolutely understand that. I also understand that life is always taking care of us.

If you're trapped in fear of dealing with areas of life outside work that are off track, I want you to think back to challenges in the past. Bring to mind the really nasty stuff that you're glad is over. Looking back, would you change anything? Most likely not. That means way back then, life was taking care of you. You didn't see it at the time, but in retrospect, you're able to see why events had to happen the way they did. No one wishes to get cancer, but we all know someone, even several people, who've had it, beat it, and state loudly they'd never go back and change the experience. What they're showing us is that the adversity eventually delivered benefits.

So what will it take for you to trust life now, in each present moment?

It may take you a while to get to a place where you authentically trust life to take care of you, so for now let's get back to the question of when work stops for the day and let's pretend you chose 2:00 p.m.

To actually step away from work at 2:00 p.m. and feel good about it, at roughly 1:30 you'll want to go through a shutdown protocol to help you transition. If you ever worked at a fast-food restaurant, do you vaguely remember going through a checklist the owner made for you at the end of the shift? It guided you through a bit of cleaning, restocking, and counting out the register, which had the effect of helping you transition out of work and into whatever you were planning on next.

In that same spirit, here's your workday shutdown checklist.

- **Acknowledge what you got done**. You may have completed all of your top three tasks and then some, or you may have finished only one of your top three. However far you got, simply acknowledge it. This is not the time to beat yourself up because you didn't get more done. The Done Before One lifestyle isn't about hyper-analyzing any one day. It's about building momentum when you wake, creating focus, taking the right action, and then looping that energy into the next day. Over time, you become unstoppable. One of my favorite affirmations when I forget this is: *I focus only on what I can do now. It's through small actions that I achieve big things.*

- **Defer, delegate, and delete the rest.** Anything you intended to do for the day that is incomplete must now be deferred to another day or delegated to another person. So, decide when you will revisit the remaining items on your list and who will be responsible for them. That may be the next day or the next week. It's only important that you decide and assign the time block on your calendar or delegate it to your teammate or staff.

  It's also possible that you decide not to do tasks on your list. As time moves on, it's only natural for some items to lose their importance or for you to change your mind. When that happens, don't hold on to old energy. Fearlessly delete what no longer needs to be done.

- **Finish tomorrow in advance.** Based on the day, what will your top three tasks be tomorrow? Remember, you should strive to never go into a workday without clarity about what you'll do. Average professionals (in other words, your competition) get to work each morning and spend half the day wrestling over what they need to do. It's no wonder they never build any momentum.

  So before you put work away each day, decide what you will do the next day. Not only will this reduce stress when you get home for the evening, but it will help you start the next day with inspiration and enthusiasm.

Imagine going into the office each day from now on knowing exactly what you'll do. Remember, you're not planning every second of the day. The goal is still to finish your top three by 1:00 p.m., which leaves plenty of time for spontaneity in the afternoon and evening.

- **Complete a digital sweep.** Go through your email, DMs, texts, and voicemails. Respond as needed and delete or defer the messages that can wait. When it comes to email, I use four primary folders: My INBOX, which is the catchall; a folder called WAITING; one called REVIEW; and one called SOMEDAY.

  When I do a digital sweep, messages I don't need to respond to get moved to one of the other three. If I'm waiting on someone else to respond, the message goes to the WAITING folder. If I need to block time to review a more in-depth message, it goes to REVIEW, and anything I don't want to deal with now but also don't want to delete goes to SOMEDAY.

  This isn't an email management book, and I understand there are people who are totally fine with 35,000 unread emails, but yours truly is not that person, so I offer my method briefly here for those who shudder at the thought of tens of thousands of messages that aren't processed.

- **Disconnect.** Now it's time to physically disconnect from work. What you need is an activity that serves as a transition between home and work. I think this is more important now than ever because we are so attached to our glowy rectangles.

When I was younger, disconnecting from work meant going to the gym. In those days, I would start my workout around 4:00 p.m., and by the time I got home, my mindset had shifted to my personal life. That was before the smartphone and before my preferred workout time changed to the morning. So these days I disconnect from work by going on an hour long walk. I like to track my steps, so I always have my iPhone and would use the time for podcasts or audiobooks.

But you know what else I caught myself doing? Tapping and scrolling social media, checking the inbox for no other reason than I could and basically getting totally lost in the device. Although I was disconnected from work, I wasn't "disconnected" in a way that would contribute to a relaxing evening.

Then I learned my iPhone would track my steps while in Airplane Mode. You don't even need a separate app. Your steps are being tracked in the Apple Health native app. I've never used an Android phone, but I bet it has this function as well. Now when I'm on my afternoon walk, my phone stays in my pocket. This was difficult at first, but there was a massive payoff.

When you truly separate yourself from both work and the digital world, your mind has space to expand in amazing ways. When not bombarded with constant stimulus from the outside, your mind can connect with infinite intelligence and receive powerful guidance from life. Creative ideas seem to spring from out of nowhere, solutions to problems come to you in amazing detail, you notice the world around you and feel grounded. The end result is a relaxed, inspired, and happy mind. Who doesn't want that?

Protect Your Evening

By the time you get home each day, you're relaxed and ready to focus on your personal and family life, right? I mean, it's easy when you come home and dinner is on the table, your spouse greets you with a smile, and your kids and pets run up to you with enthusiasm. That's not your life, you say? Okay, so it's not the 1950s anymore, but wouldn't it be nice if that scene played out for you at least a couple of days a week?

Well, whatever your life is like outside work, kids or no kids, pets or no pets, married or single, you deserve to enjoy it, and in today's world, just like every other part of the day, if you don't design how your evenings will go, the rest of the world will do it for you by default. You might be tempted to gloss over this section as it may seem less important than morning and daily productivity routines, but just like every athlete knows they'll suffer without proper rest, so will you.

Remember, you're on power save mode at this point and sleep is how you'll fully recharge for the next day. If your evening is a hectic mess, you won't sleep well and won't wake up with a full charge. No amount of coffee will overcome that deficit. To protect your evening, you'll use one mental and one physical technique.

Leave It on the Hook: The Mental Technique

The mental technique is called leaving it on the hook. This practice helps you resist the temptation to reconnect with work.

Long ago, when my real estate sales career took off, I could easily spend all day on the phone. Again, this was before the smartphone, texting was a pain on early mobile phones, so everyone called everyone else about everything. It became common for me to walk into the house each evening finishing up the call I'd started in the car. Of course, my intent was to finish up quickly; I'd even announce to the person on the phone, loud enough for everyone at home to hear me, that I'd just walked into my house and needed to wrap it up. I guess that made me feel better as I sat in my home office for another thirty minutes to an hour—sometimes longer.

It didn't take long for my little family, comprising my partner, Jon, and our two pups, to stop greeting me when I got home. To this day I'm not entirely sure how long this went on, but I'll never forget the day I got home and, for the first time in years, walked in not on the phone. I was totally ignored—even by the dogs! The truth is, I'd conditioned my family to ignore me when I got home. Humans are one thing, but dogs have it in their DNA to run up to their owners after they've been away, or so I thought. I felt sick to my stomach and guilty as hell. Was this part of the price of success?

Thankfully, I've always had world-class mentors. The next day I brought this up to one of them who told me, "Jasen, your family doesn't care about what happens at work and your clients don't care what happens at home. You need to learn to keep them separate so you can be fully present with both."

When I asked how to separate the two worlds, he told me to imagine I had two bags, one for work and one for home, that hung from hooks in my garage. The rule was I could only carry one bag at a time. When I left the house each morning, he told me to visualize putting my personal life bag on an imaginary hook and picking up my work bag. Then all day while at work, when tempted to think about, worry over, or otherwise deal with my personal life, to remind myself that I couldn't because I don't have that bag with me. I was to stay focused on the needs of my clients.

Then, when I got home, he told me to visualize putting my work bag on the hook and picking up my home bag. When tempted to think about, worry over, or otherwise deal with issues at work, to remind myself that I couldn't because I didn't have the work bag with me anymore. I was to stay focused on my family, friends, and personal life.

This particular mentor was the best salesperson I've ever met and taught me with visuals. There never was a literal hook in my garage or outside my home office door, but to this day I'll still catch myself subtly lifting my arm like I'm switching bags on the hook. I doubt anyone would notice it at this point, but the muscle memory is definitely there. In case you missed the visual, if you work from home, the hook you envision should be outside the door to your home office. In retrospect, an actual hook might have been a great idea. Possibly even a funny conversation starter when guests came over.

When I learned this technique, I wasn't thinking with a Done Before One mindset, but it certainly aligned with the philosophy I was building. My mentor was trying to teach me to stay present in the moment. He knew how futile (and unfortunately common) it was to go to the office and worry about home, then go home and worry about the office. With that mindset, you're not giving your best to anyone. Don't your clients and coworkers deserve you at your best? Doesn't your family? Even if you're single or without kids and your "family" is just an extended family of friends, don't they deserve you at your best? Think of the last time you told those important to you that you're going to take a call and "it'll just be a minute." Was it just one of those 1,440 minutes? I doubt it.

The good news is that if you can train your family to ignore you, you can train them to reconnect. Start by leaving work on the hook when you come home. Imagine how much easier this will be when you've completed your most important tasks before 1:00 p.m. Everything else you did before you got home is a bonus, so you'll feel less pressure to reconnect with work in the evening.

Giving someone your undivided attention is the most impactful gift you have to give. Picture your family watching you ignore a call or, better yet, ignoring your glowy rectangles (all of them, iPad and laptop too) and instead focusing on them. It's a mindset shift for sure and it's a decision you have to make. For better or for worse, are you going to engage fully with the other parts of your life or hide from them?

Evening Journal: The Physical Technique

I'm going to assume you said "engage fully" when asked how you want to interact with your family, so you'll need one more critical tool: an old-school paper journal. While you can leave work on the hook when you're done for the day, you can't always control when you have thoughts about work. You should expect to have thoughts about activities you need to do the next day and various other ideas you'd like to remember.

Most people simply try to remember, which would be okay if you only ever had one thought enter your mind about the next day, but we all know that's not the case. When you hear people say they can't sleep because they can't shut off their mind, what they're telling you is that they've had too many thoughts about the next day and are trying to keep it all in order in their mind—and are likely worrying about forgetting something.

The evening journal is the perfect solution because, whenever you have one of those thoughts, it gives you a trusted place to record the thought and let it go. The journal will be there for you in the morning, so there's no reason to hold on to the thought. Each time a new thought enters your mind, grab the journal, write it down, and move on.

You can even do this when you're actively engaged with your family. Simply let them in on the secret. Tell them that in order to stay present with them, when you have intrusive thoughts about work, they'll see you silently grab the journal to record the thoughts and get them out of your head so you can remain present.

One big key is to make sure you don't use a glowy rectangle for this. It's just not worth the risk of getting caught up in it. Find a paper journal you like and leave the phone on the charger. The biggest benefit of the journal is that the longer you stay disconnected from work, the more space your subconscious mind has to work on tough problems throughout the evening. Don't be surprised if, once you get in the habit of using an evening journal, you start generating all kinds of creative solutions and new ideas seemingly out of the blue. The truth is that they were always there for you, but you're no longer blocking them.

Turn Big Challenges Over to Life: Use Your Angel Army

Using an evening journal can go a long way toward keeping your mind clear and free of worrying thoughts as you near bedtime, but what if you're facing a bigger challenge? If you just lost your biggest client, jotting down the continuous stream of negative emotions you're likely feeling throughout the evening can help, even if it only temporarily gets them out of your head, but it may not be enough to prevent you from tossing and turning in bed all night. Sometimes you need to call in the big-league experts.

Have you ever struggled with a problem all day and night only to wake up the next morning with the solution staring you right in the face? If so, you've unconsciously used one of my favorite problem-solving techniques: you turned the challenge over to life. You could also say you turned it over to your subconscious mind, the universe, gave it up to god, or placed it on the altar. To me, those are all ways of saying the same thing. Whatever label you use, each night we have an opportunity to work with our most powerful resource.

Dr. Wayne Dyer used to warn us about dwelling on negative thoughts before bed because he knew our subconscious mind would pick up on the negativity and marinate in it for hours as we slept. This can happen even if you're using an evening journal and especially if you're dealing with an issue causing intense negative emotions. Turning the issue and all the nasty feeling emotions attached to it over to life is a strategy you'll come to love.

Even if the challenge you face isn't negative but simply complex, you can use life to give you a big assist. You've likely done this by accident before, so here's how to make it deliberate. As soon as you crawl into bed, think about the challenge weighing you down. Then, ask life to work on the solution overnight while you are sleeping.

Once you ask for help, you have to let it go. If you lie there and continue to dwell on the problem, you're only getting in the way, so when your emotions are particularly intense, you might need a sleep aid like a meditation app with sleep tracks. I use the Headspace app when I don't want to risk dwelling on the problem I've asked life to solve.

The best thing about this technique is that you can use it every night. Lately, rather than turning my bigger challenges over to life, I've been getting more specific and calling on my angel army. My angel army comprises all the people and pets who were once a part of my life and are no longer here physically. Their bodies died, but their spirits are still present and accessible as a part of the energy of the universe. I even have people who harmed me in my army, like my physically and emotionally abusive stepfather. It makes sense to me that once all the baggage of his human experience was gone, my once-evil stepdad, who now exists on a higher energy plane without his human baggage, would love to help.

So now every night I call upon my angel army and ask them for all kinds of guidance. It's almost inexplicable, but literally every time they've come through. Their ways of delivering help vary from fresh ideas and inspiration when I wake to "chance meetings" the next day.

Even if you're skeptical, you now have two choices: go to bed like most people do and let your mind stew on whatever it was you were stewing on all evening or use your mind as the tool it is and see what happens when you turn your challenges over to life.

Charge Your Mind, Use Your Mind, Empty Your Mind

The Done Before One lifestyle, when executed fully as intended, forms an energetic loop that takes all the momentum and progress generated in a day and feeds it into the next day. If you string seven of those days together, you'll have experienced a productive and fulfilling week. String four weeks together and you should begin seeing clear evidence of the power of this way of being. String three months together and you should see a measurable impact on your mindset, your production, and your pocketbook. From there, the sky's the limit.

This energetic loop works so well because it provides the method to charge your mind, use your mind, and empty your mind daily. The morning routine picks up where sleep left off to fill your mind with intention and inspiration. All the work you do to get Done Before One is where you most intensely use your mind. When you finish your day strong, you are allowing your mind to empty all the way to the point of sleep, where the refilling (recharging) process begins again.

All three are essential to a Done Before One life. If your mind isn't full of energy and inspiration, you won't be able to use it effectively. Emptying your mind enough for it to relax and recharge overnight sets the stage for optimal performance the following day.

To ensure our digital devices operate at optimum performance, software works to regulate the lithium-ion batteries such that they stay in a range between full charge and power save mode. The software helps keep the batteries from overcharging and from being completely drained. Both extremes will shorten the life of the battery. That sounds like a human mind to me. Too much charge, not so healthy. Being frequently drained to exhaustion? Not good either.

To continue the tech analogy, a mind looping back and forth from green to yellow and touching on red before recharging is the daily pattern that leads to an optimal life. Then, at intervals, it helps to do a little software update. The next chapter will show you how to do a software update for your mind.

7

THE POWER OF THE FORECAST

With regular weekly forecasting in place, you'll never again walk into the office on a Monday without knowing what you're going to do.

The Cure for Sunday Scaries

The phrase "weekend blues" was commonly used in American culture during the 1970s. At that time, "weekend blues" was used to describe people who suffered from intense loneliness on the weekend and who would commonly sink into depression.

In fact, in those days, the highest number of suicide attempts occurred Saturday evening and on Sunday. People believed that the structure provided by a 9-to-5 job or school kept individuals engaged with life, but when that structure was lifted on the weekend, these people didn't know how to handle their lives. I was too young for any of this to register, but in the 1970s, the US was suffering from stagflation—an economy with both high unemployment and soaring inflation. Is this is why people felt so bad when they weren't at work?

We successfully overcame stagflation and then the oil bust in the 1980s, and by the time I entered the workforce in the early 1990s, the economy was moving towards a massive recovery. Still, a *New York Times* article claimed the weekend blues were back, but this time they used the term "Sunday blues." People were reportedly no longer depressed all weekend, but Sunday was still a problem. Clearly, something shifted. Was it that the economy needed to fully recover before we'd be able to enjoy the full weekend?

Apparently not. More recently, we've been using the term "Sunday scaries," which first appeared in the Urban Dictionary in 2009 and was used to describe the feeling of being so hung over on Sunday you ended up questioning your life choices.

The use of the term quickly transformed into the equivalent of the "Sunday blues," but now people used it regardless of whether they had consumed alcohol over the weekend. One definition I found of Sunday scaries is "the irrational fear and internal darkness that overcomes you on Sundays, when the impending doom of Monday is right around the corner."

Dramatic much? When I first read that, I wondered, do people really feel that way? No matter how good the economy gets?

A widely quoted study by LinkedIn found that 80 percent of the American workforce reports feeling some level of the Sunday scaries. The number soars to 91 percent for millennials and 94 percent for Gen Z, so it might seem that we are becoming increasingly incapable of handling the simple act of getting back to work on Monday. What is really causing this?

It doesn't take long to find a wide range of opinions. Drinking too much alcohol is one cause that most seem to agree on. Alcohol dehydrates the body, deprives your brain and other organs of much needed glucose, and throws off the balance of your neurotransmitters. Alcohol suppresses glutamate, which causes brain activity to slow while also increasing the effects of GABA, similar to drugs like Xanax and Valium. That's why a drink or glass of wine at night takes the edge off the day.

At the same time, alcohol increases dopamine levels, which activates the reward center of your brain and makes you feel great. So you keep drinking to get the dopamine hit, which masks what's happening to your brain. That's why the next day, a hangover comes with a feeling of depression. If you drink too much, it can take several days for your brain to rebalance neurotransmitters like glutamate, GABA, and dopamine.

So that's part of the story and the easiest to fix. Unless you have a serious addiction, just cut back on the alcohol. But half of the people responding to LinkedIn's survey didn't drink on the weekend. Some blamed capitalism as the problem, claiming we live in an overly materialistic and profit-driven society. Others blamed class insecurity, a feeling of having to work harder for less and never making any progress. One person in the study claimed to be so busy at work that Saturday was the only day to catch up, leaving Sunday as his only day of leisure. In my opinion, most of this is hyperbole.

People undoubtedly feel the way they report or are totally convinced capitalism is a problem, but holding on to those beliefs is just not beneficial for them in any way. The more I searched, the more I could find people overdramatizing their situation and simultaneously blaming everyone but themselves.

Other than cutting back on alcohol, common cures offered for the Sunday scaries are often nonspecific, such as seeking joy, practicing meditation, or keeping a normal sleep schedule. One company claims 3:28 p.m. on Sunday is the inflection point when most people start to feel the scaries. Of course, they sell CBD gummies and recommend you take them starting at 3:28 p.m. These clearly aren't the folks who are blaming capitalism.

Psychologists label Sunday scaries as anticipatory anxiety, which puts people in fight-or-flight mode. This causes a flood of adrenaline and cortisol throughout the body, preventing a good night's sleep. They recommend cognitive-behavioral ther- apy as the solution, which is guided, of course, by a therapist.

The silliest, but most creative solution I've read is to extend the feeling of the weekend into the week, basically turning the calendar into one long, never-ending weekend. With this solu- tion, it's suggested you schedule something fun each day. Monday movie night, taco Tuesday with friends, hump day happy hour, Thursday dinner parties, and then before you know it, TGIF! I don't know about you, but that sounds exhausting.

Truth be told, I'm not against any of these proposed solu- tions to the Sunday scaries, I just don't think they're needed. Certainly, one should seek joy, keep a normal sleep schedule, meditate, and limit alcohol consumption to improve overall health. Therapy and CBD gummies or both are great if that helps you live a better life and, of course, who doesn't love taco Tuesday. But do we need all this coping just to fight back negative emotions on Sunday? It seems we've simply failed for several generations now to teach people how to cope with life. In my opinion, there's a better way.

The most powerful cure for the Sunday scaries lies in the Weekly Forecast.

The Weekly Forecast

Contained Chaos

How often do you clean your house? I'm referring to the frequency at which you perform a thorough cleaning of your house, including scrubbing the bathrooms and kitchen, washing the linens, mopping the floors, and dusting everything. Most people I know do this, or have it done, once a week.

In my days as an active Realtor, I went into other people's homes almost daily and learned quickly that not everyone has the same definition of clean. I also learned that the condition of a person's home reflects their state of mind and their life. It was nearly universally true that when I was working with a home that was consistently messy, dirty, or chaotic, the owner's mindset and life were also messy, dirty, and chaotic.

Thankfully, finding a home in that state was the exception, not the rule. For most families I'd work with, the regular clean-up ritual contained the chaos created by living life during the week. Your home can be messy for only so long before you must either clean it up or feel the negative effects.

Likewise, taking time out to clean your "work house" on a weekly basis pays big dividends. Except, unlike your home, you can't hire anyone to do this for you. Work gets messy and chaotic, too, especially if you're pushing yourself to grow in your profession. Sometimes chaos is a good sign because it means you're trying new things, but if you don't clean up at intervals, that same chaos weighs on you and drag down your effectiveness, production, and eventually your income.

The Weekly Forecast process is how you clean up your professional life. It's a structured process that guides you through a review of your week and, more importantly, helps you set intentions for the week ahead. With regular weekly forecasting in place, you'll never again walk into the office on a Monday without knowing what you're going to do. Because you've already made those decisions, anxiety plummets, especially on Sunday afternoon.

But it's not just Monday. When you do a Weekly Forecast, you're finishing the entire week before you even start. Remember, the Done Before One lifestyle is about controlling your day until 1:00 p.m., then letting the afternoon fall apart and get chaotic if it must. As long as you control the next day until 1:00 p.m., you contain the chaos. It works the same with a weekly timeframe.

Over the course of a week, tasks that you eventually need to deal with build up while you remain focused on your most important work. That's natural and not a sign of failure. Strengthening the habit of remaining focused on what you determine to be important is, in fact, a sign of success. Now, assuming your work requires you to interact with other humans, you can expect them to try to pull you off track, distract you, or just not do what you need them to do in order to move forward.

In other words, working with other people can be messy and chaotic. They have their own agendas and timelines, and those won't always line up with yours. But as long as you have a regularly scheduled time to step back and breathe, other people won't bother you so much.

Complete Your Circles

The Weekly Forecast gives you a chance to complete your circles. When I am coaching entrepreneurs, I often find I need to help them build the discipline to finish what they started. When you work for yourself, it's natural to become overwhelmed with the large number of projects on your plate. The more business you have, the more of an issue this becomes because, when you're self-employed, you're always managing various projects that are moving along on separate time frames.

Sometimes when I'm speaking to a group of business owners, I'll ask if they want to see me quickly draw an image of a crazy person. I'm sure they're expecting me to draw something like a caricature of a person with messy hair, but instead I draw a bunch of incomplete circles at various angles. It looks like I just wrote the letter C multiple times. Then I trace those open circles as I describe someone doing a typical task before interrupting themselves to jump to something else. It sounds like this:

"Okay, I'm going to dedicate a solid hour to prospecting today, BING, oh crap I need to respond to this client's text message, where did they send that email attachment, DING, oh wow Saks is having a great sale, I wonder if they included the shoes I've been wanting." Hey office mate, how was your weekend? Oh, you went to a fun wedding? That reminds me, I need to find a new photographer to help us create posts for social media. Hahaha, hey check out this meme. Lunch? Sure I could do that, where should we go?"

I could go on literally all day, but do you see what I mean? We all have plenty around us to keep our minds permanently distracted. Our attention can become so scattered that our days become a bunch of incomplete circles. As an entrepreneur, you're smart and talented and you have big goals, but you can't go weeks on end feeling busy but making no forward progress. That will definitely make you feel crazy.

Controlling your day until 1:00 p.m. while staying focused on your daily top three tasks will be a tremendous help in completing your most important circles, and completing your circles is how you stay focused. You can use the Weekly Forecast to help you complete any remaining circles that you actually want to finish. Naturally, completing circles and tying up loose ends at regular intervals will also help reduce stress and anxiety.

Thinking about Work vs. Doing Work

We can't overstate the importance of taking action. Getting stuck in paralysis from analysis is something we all should look to avoid, but that doesn't mean slowing down and thinking about your work isn't also important. When you spend an excessive amount of time obsessing over one thing, you get stuck and risk never making a decision or taking action. But giving yourself time to think broadly about what you're doing and making sure you're in alignment with your goals is critical.

During the Weekly Forecast, you have time to slow down and think consciously about your professional and personal life. At this slower pace, you can make decisions that can keep your actions in alignment with your bigger vision or, when necessary, correct actions that are pulling you away from it. The more the outside world fights for your attention, the more you need regular and deliberately held space to go within and answer the question: Am I doing what I need to do to live the life I'm telling myself I want to live?

The Weekly Forecast Process

The Weekly Forecast has five basic steps:

1. Record your wins.
2. Review your performance.
3. Clear the decks.
4. Review your projects and goals.
5. Incorporate your personal life.

Although there's no rule on how long you should spend going through those steps, in my experience, it takes at the very least ninety minutes. Obviously, when you've got more going on, it could take longer. In any case, you should be willing to spend whatever time to do the high-level thinking about your business and life required to get the outcome you want.

For a long time, Friday was my forecast day and lately it's shifted to Saturday afternoon. If you've never done anything like this before, use your instincts and pick the day you feel you'll most likely be able to lock out the world and go through the five steps. When you pick your day, commit to it for at least three months. You'll see why soon, but for now, trust me when I say consistency is key to building this important habit.

Step One: Record Your Wins

So you've picked your day, and the time has come to forecast the coming week. You don't need any special tools. Whatever combination of journals, planners, goal-setting, and tracking tools you use is fine. With those in front of you, begin thinking about what went well for you during the week and record your wins somewhere. Achievement-oriented people are exceptional at beating themselves up over what went wrong or what didn't get done and are generally lousy at acknowledging the progress made in the recent past.

Being hard on yourself may sound virtuous, but the older I get, the more I realize the importance of one of the ten principles: a true master of self never uses words against himself. The world will provide plenty of criticism without your help, so one way to hold more of your power is to develop a stubborn refusal to beat yourself up. At some point, you have to understand criticism will help nothing and, in fact, does plenty of harm. How could you build enthusiasm for the next week if you berate yourself over the one that just passed?

When you start your Weekly Forecast by recording your wins, you build a success-based narrative in your mind. That doesn't mean you'll ignore issues that need to be corrected; it means when you get to those items, you'll be in a more powerful state of mind to handle them.

When I'm recording my wins, I don't limit myself to any specific number. Most preprinted planners I've seen have sections somewhere that guide you to list three to five positives. I'm less interested in the number than I am in the feeling generated by making the list. Before I do anything else, my intention is to pump myself up and so I'll stay on this step until I honestly feel good.

Often the wins I'm recording are similar or even exactly the same as the week before. For example, when I write a book, there are several weeks where one of my wins is "I completed my daily writing before 1:00 p.m." When I finish the book, that win drops off the list. I also include wins from my personal life like improvements in my tennis game, sticking to my nutrition plan, and not getting lost in my glowy rectangle in the evening.

When you are going through a particularly difficult time, keep your wins general and broad in scope. Maybe your workouts were crap this week, but you still won because you made it to the gym five days in a row. Maybe you completely blew it at work, but you still won because you haven't given up. Maybe you spent all week prospecting for new clients and have no appointments to show for it, but you still won because you put in the time. Maybe instead of losing weight, you gained some, but you still won because you allowed yourself to celebrate your friend's birthday. Maybe your entire week was a huge flaming turd of a mess, but you still won because you woke up, you're still breathing, and you still have the ingredients to make waffles!

You know you're ready to move on to the next step when you feel light and in a state of appreciation. Again, this isn't about making excuses for yourself or glossing over tasks that need attention. It's about establishing a narrative in your mind that puts you in a positive and powerful state. From that positive state, you can take action to improve. At the end of the day, you're the one responsible for your state of being anyway.

Step Two: Review Your Performance

Okay, so you pumped yourself up. Now it's time to review your performance over the last week honestly. What went well? What didn't? Where was your head? When it comes to your measurable goals, how far did you get?

To answer these questions, you can look back at your journal, and if you don't keep one, this is a perfect reason to start. Rereading what you wrote over the course of the week can give you insight into how you've been thinking. Glance at your calendar over the past week for reminders of what you did and revisit your daily top three tasks. Look at your sales reports and total up your expenses to monitor the numbers.

When you look back with these prompts, you're able to take an honest account of what you actually did all week.

Remember, as you review the past, there's nothing you can change and therefore no point in slipping back into self-criticism. But bringing your performance, good or bad, to the front of your mind allows you to make some proactive decisions for the next week. Based on your actions, what changes or adjustments need to be made for the coming week?

You could determine you need to spend more time developing referrals and less time going out to lunch. Or realize you're losing too much time talking at the gym and need to stay more focused. Whatever it is, write it down so you can see it in black and white. No one else is going to see this, so be honest with yourself.

Think of reviewing your performance as giving yourself feedback like a coach would. A good coach helps you look at your recent performance and, rather than tell you what you should do, offers feedback to help you make your own decisions for improvement. That way, you take ownership of the situation. There's no reason you can't do this for yourself. Once you've objectively looked at your performance and recorded your analysis, set it aside so you can clear the decks (close those open circles) before committing to anything new the next week.

Step Three: Clear the Decks

The third step in the Weekly Forecast can be controversial because there seem to be two kinds of people in the world: one who gets to inbox zero regularly and another whose number of unread messages has a comma in it. Although no one is ever at inbox zero for more than a few minutes, it's not that hard to keep your inbox clean most of the time. These days, our inboxes contain most of our incomplete circles.

First, let's expand the definition of inbox. When I say inbox, I mean any place that collects incoming communication, including notes you make for yourself. Certainly that includes your email inbox, but it also includes your other digital inboxes like social media DMs, text messages, and voicemails. It also includes any paper-based communication you have, such as snail mail, office memos, and notes you jot down for yourself. If the dominance of digital communication has caused you to end up without an inbox for snail mail and other papers, do yourself a favor and get one. Your inboxes, paper included, are your trusted places to collect all your clutter throughout the week.

To clear your inboxes, you go through each of these spaces and make rapid-fire decisions. If you can act upon or respond to a message in under five minutes, do it now. If it's going to take much longer than that, you'll need to dedicate a block of time on your calendar. Move messages like that to a folder called REVIEW. If you come across something that needs to be delegated, forward it to the person who'll be helping you and move the original note to a folder called WAITING. If something is trash, hit delete, and if you come across something you don't want to delete but don't have to take action on anytime soon, move it to a folder called SOMEDAY.

So now, for digital and paper inboxes (for paper you can use file folders), you have the following folders:

- **INBOX:** This is where incoming messages collect initially.
- **REVIEW:** This is where you find tasks that need blocks of time assigned to them in order to get them done.
- **WAITING:** This is where you find everything that needs action to be taken by someone else, whether or not you delegated it, before you can move forward.
- **SOMEDAY:** This is where you keep notes you'd rather not delete, but don't want or need to deal with right away.

As you can see, clearing your inboxes is less about getting to inbox zero and more about containing the chaos that naturally builds over time. You are far less likely to stress over the unimportant things everyone else does if you build trust with yourself around this practice. For example, when you remain focused on your top three tasks for the day, emails will go unanswered, requests for your time will be unmet, and you're going to have to get used to temporarily ignoring the requests that aren't important or urgent. Many people who are conditioned to react to the world and have no system they can trust to respond to it get freaked out by that.

But remember, we build trust with consistency over time, even when it comes to trusting ourselves. If you commit to the forecasting process and stick with it for at least three months, you'll have showed that you can trust yourself—at least on this topic. Then, because you know for sure you have dedicated time to keep yourself on track, you'll be able to relax and focus on the items that truly make your business and personal life better. You'll stop reacting and start responding.

Even better, people will start seeing you as reliable, trustworthy, and hyper-productive. It's sad to say, but because most people don't run their life this way, it's increasingly easy to become known as the person who gets shit done.

Step Four: Review Quarterly Goals and Projects

Now, with your professional house clean, it's time to review your quarterly goals and current projects. One of the most impactful lessons I ever learned from my mentors was the importance of viewing everything as a project. School teaches us the opposite. As we grow up, we learn to work linearly until we finally graduate and enter a world that unfortunately hasn't moved along in a linear fashion for a long time.

Starting in real estate made this concept easier to grasp because each buyer or seller was literally a different project with its own folder. The people involved with one transaction were separate from the others and each moved along at its own pace. As my business grew, I realized that every substantial goal I wanted to accomplish was a project. We also call them goals, but goals are what we hit when we break them down into small steps—and all those small steps add up to a project.

I had goals for marketing, implementing technology, increasing referral business, and winning company awards. I accomplished all of those goals by completing a series of projects made up of individual tasks.

You might be surprised how many times in private coaching I work with people who don't think that way. It's a simple concept, but by now you should see exactly why a person without the control afforded by a Done Before One lifestyle moves through the day reacting, which leaves them no mental space to deliberately align their projects with their goals.

Let's just assume that you have clearly defined quarterly goals and projects that you're working on, regardless of whether you have considered the connection between your projects and goals. Each goal and project should have a clearly defined outcome. If not, you'll never know if you actually finish the project or hit the goal. And of course it should have a deadline. Goals without deadlines are just dreams. Projects without deadlines are how the government wastes all our money.

So when reviewing your goals and projects, this part of the forecast is as simple as looking at your intended outcome and answering one question: What is the next task that must happen to move forward? All of your power lies in consistent execution of the simple, small steps. Affirm: I focus only on what I can do now. It's through small actions that I achieve big results.

So what is it that needs to happen next? If your project is about marketing, the next action could be to create a video or take the photos needed. If your project is increasing referral business, your next action could be to call all of your past clients from the last quarter. If your project is to lose weight, the next action could be to schedule interviews with personal trainers who can help you.

When you go through all of your goals and projects, you'll end up with a list of "things to do" next. It's from this list that you'll derive your top three most important tasks for the next week. The average performer, if they even get this far, will attempt in vain to complete the entire to-do list, starting with the easiest tasks because, of course, it feels better and can be claimed as legitimate work. But when living a Done Before One life, it is necessary to thoughtfully consider this list.

As you think about your list, which three are the most important to get done in the coming week? I know, I know, they're all important. But from your point of view, to stand in integrity with yourself, which three must get done? Fill in the blanks: "It's next Friday night and I feel like a million bucks because if nothing else, I completed _____, _____ and _____."

Most weeks, you'll be able to negotiate with yourself and identify the three most important tasks from your sizable list. But there will also be times when there are only two critical activities, or even one very critical task that must get done. When that happens, allow yourself to zero in on those one or two items. It doesn't always have to be three. Fewer is totally cool, but if you go over three, I'd question if you're being honest with yourself.

Your weekly top three will be broken down into smaller tasks that will fill your days. For example, if one of your tasks is to build an agenda for an upcoming meeting, you may need to research topics of discussion, gather materials for the meeting, confirm speakers, and more. Now you have not only your weekly top three, but a more granular list of specific steps. From that list, determine Monday's top three and block your calendar.

This is what so many people miss. Each item on your list takes time to accomplish, so when will you spend the time? It can't be whenever you get to it. You must make the decision. These time blocks become appointments, even if you're the only one there. For example, you may decide that Monday from 9:00 a.m. to 10:00 a.m. you have an appointment (with yourself) to call your past clients from last quarter.

As soon as you make this decision, the universe will hear and test you to see if you mean it. It won't be long before someone asks you to do something on Monday at 9:00 a.m. It's in that moment where you have the opportunity to build trust with yourself. Do you react and change your plans and thereby teach yourself that you don't mean what you say, that your decisions aren't important, or do you say, "Can't then, I'm booked"?

In any case, once you've made it this far, you've forecasted your week and won't have to spend Sunday worrying about Monday. Monday is already done. You just have to show up and do what you said you'd do. But there's one more thing to consider when finishing up your Weekly Forecast: your personal life.

Step Five: Integrate Your Personal Life

It's normal to go through the forecasting process with a heavy emphasis on your professional life. Your personal life can benefit from this as well. For all the talk of work/life balance in the world, I've found no one who has legitimately achieved it for more than a day or so. The whole concept of work/life balance seems to pit one against the other, forcing us to pick a winner.

If work wins too frequently, marriages fall apart, friendships dissolve, physical health suffers, and pets get neglected. If the personal life wins too frequently, your career advancement stops, professional talents don't get developed, customers suffer, your bank account dwindles, and often your sense of self-worth takes a beating.

A better way to look at this is to use the word *integration*. The Done Before One lifestyle helps you integrate your personal and professional lives if for no other reason than you've taken control of how you're spending your time on the planet and can literally see space on your calendar (after 1:00 p.m.) to integrate other parts of your life. So before you wrap up your Weekly Forecast, look for ways to integrate your personal life.

If you like to read and have a stack of books you'd like to catch up on, when could you schedule an appointment for that? That recipe you've been wanting to try? Which night could you plan that? The Italian lessons you've been meaning to start? When's that appointment? That precious pup who is sitting at home yearning for you to throw the ball? When will you schedule an appointment for him?

Look, I know it sounds cold initially, but when you look at everything in your life as an appointment, you'll understand how important it is to be as deliberate about how you spend your time as you are about how you spend your money.

The Weekly Time Budget

When I was a kid, I used to watch as my mom would balance her checkbook at the end of the week. Of course, as a young child, that activity meant little, but when I was old enough, my dad helped me get my own checking account. Suddenly, I understood why balancing the checkbook was necessary. Without smartphones and the internet, it was the only way to keep tabs on how I spent money and forced me to take a good look at the balance.

The younger you are, the more likely you may feel that you have almost limitless time and focus less on accumulating money. Of course, as you age, that dynamic shifts. You may have money but place much more value on time. The sooner you can reach the place where you truly understand time as more valuable than money, the better. After all, you can generate as much cash as you like, but when it comes to time, the best you can do is use your money to buy freedom to use the time you have on activities and items you find enjoyable.

When going through your Weekly Forecast, reviewing your calendar from the past week is a little like balancing your checkbook or combing through your cash flow statement. You're looking back in time at what has already been spent and making decisions on how you'll move forward. But you're an entrepreneur, so you also likely have at least one financial budget.

The Weekly Time Budget exercise works just like a financial budget. It guides you as you make expenditures and raises your awareness of moments when you're getting off track. If you're used to doing quarterly financial budgets for your business, creating time budgets should be no problem for you.

The Weekly Time Budget is a visualization exercise where you're spending the ideal amount of time on each area of life that is important to you. Imagine a week where everyone cooperates with you. Your coworkers do what they're supposed to do, your clients follow your advice, your kids do what you ask them to do, your spouse does nothing but support you and pump you up, you make every green light, hit every workout, complete your weekly top three and have time for yourself. Sounds amazing, doesn't it? Well, unless you're willing to visualize your week in that way, it'll never happen.

I'm not suggesting every week will, or even should, be the same. But most of them can be close to ideal if you lay out how you intend to spend your time, just like you do with a budget for your money. Here are the steps to creating your Weekly Time Budget:

Step 1: Lay out one blank week at a glance and block out your day off. Which day will you set aside to completely disconnect from your professional life? If you want to be at your best at work, you need at least one twenty-four-hour period each week where you recharge. Trust me, two half days won't cut it. One full day away from all work-related activities is what you need.

When I was a young salesperson, I chose Sunday for no other reason than it sounded good. My mentor warned me that as soon as I picked a day, life would test me. Sure enough, the first week I took Sunday off, someone offered me the opportunity to host a hot open house. So I declined the invitation and told the agent it was my day off. Haha! I'm only kidding. I did the open house and then, when no one came through, I beat myself up in the evening for not doing what my mentor asked me to do.

Eventually, you learn people don't take regular time off because of a scarcity mindset. What if I missed out on a client? I'm sure that's what I was thinking when I agreed to do the open house. And at that point, I certainly needed the money. But I'll say it again: one client more or less, in the long run, won't make or break anyone. The inability to take time to recharge, however, will burn you out and lead to a resentment of your own career.

My advice to you is to pick a day you know you want and are reasonably sure you can keep consistent. Then expect life to test you to see if you really mean it. When someone wants you to do anything you don't want to do on your day off, just say, "Can't then, I'm booked."

As long as you are consistent, it won't take long before people respect your boundary. You'll get text messages, emails, and voicemails that begin with, "I'm so sorry to bother you on your day off. Please don't respond. I just needed to leave you this message so I didn't forget."

Step 2: Block out your morning routine. If you go to the gym first thing in the morning, block that out. Is it Monday through Friday? What about the weekend? I know some people who keep their morning routine seven days a week; whereas, I have different weekday and weekend routines. My weekday routines, as you know, build momentum into the workday, but my weekend morning routines set the tone for a more relaxed day.

For example, on Saturday and Sunday mornings, I get up one hour later. A whole hour! I know I'm such a lazy bum. After going to the gym on Saturday, I go to the farmers' market. My reward for getting those errands done is enjoying a solo Saturday brunch. That's my time to go to my favorite restaurant and just be alone after a week of interacting with many people. Sunday mornings, I start by walking for ninety minutes while listening to Joel Osteen's sermon. That's how I stay prayed up! Which is funny because I wasn't raised with any religious doctrine. But I cannot listen to Joel without feeling uplifted and full of hope. When working on your own time budget, build in activities that make you feel like I feel listening to Joel.

Step 3: Block out your prime work hours. This is the time after your morning routine ends until 1:00 p.m. of course. We already discussed that some days you'll go beyond 1:00, but what we're budgeting here is your prime time, when you produce your best work.

Step 4: Block out your personal and family time. Besides your morning routine, what other activities do you regularly spend time on that should be budgeted? Afternoon walks, recreational sports, playing instruments, learning languages—in other words, your hobbies. If you do them regularly (or have always wanted to do them), block them out. During the year I'm writing this, I have Italian lessons blocked for an hour each weekday afternoon on my time budget. Also, on Friday late morning I have tennis practice. Then, of course, there are family obligations. If you have kids, block out the ideal or most likely time for taking them to practice, games, and school events. Or if you are caring for an elderly parent. In that case, don't forget to block out time for visiting and medical appointments.

Step 5: Leave white space. The point of this exercise isn't to budget every second of time. You're going to want some time "in the bank," so to speak, especially in the afternoon for unexpected events that come up, and I don't think I have to convince you that plenty will come up.

An exercise like the Weekly Time Budget does a great job of showing you just how little time you have to spend each week. Again, we can generate as much cash as we need, but none of us can do that with time. We all get the same amount of it each week and how we spend it has a huge effect on our life experience.

Some people spend their time as if life is a dress rehearsal. It would be a shame for you to work so hard at learning to be Done Before One, only to blow the week overall. The whole point of a Done Before One lifestyle is to give you guilt-free access to the rest of your time during the week. Don't squander it. Use this exercise to practice spending your time deliberately. Then, once per quarter, as you grow and change, you can revisit your budget and make adjustments as needed.

Quarterly and Annual Forecasts

You might have noticed that we're moving in the reverse order of most systems that fall into the time management/goal-setting category. That's because if you don't get control of your days, they won't add up to your quarterly goals, let alone any bigger annual goals.

Did you know there's a day for quitters? It's called National Quitters Day, and it falls on the second Friday in January. This started in 2019 and is based on a study by a social networking site for athletes. They determined that a whopping 80 percent of people gave up on their fitness-based goals (or resolutions) by the second Friday of the year.

I see the same thing in business every year. We start out with big statements like "This is the year I get it together and make real money," "This is my year to be the top producer," or "This is the year I'll start the business, write the book, change careers, and on and on." While people may not admit to giving up on those kinds of goals by the second Friday of the year, when they actually give up isn't far off.

Dreaming up and expressing big goals is fun and feels amazing. The problem, as we are discovering, is that talking about big goals gives people enough of a hit of excitement that they become unconsciously satisfied. Researchers call this the intention-behavior gap or the difference between what we say we intend to do and what we actually do. It seems the more we talk about our goals, the wider the gap becomes.

This is completely the opposite of what early mentors told me. Establish a goal and then tell everyone they advised me. That way you'll hold yourself accountable, which was another way of suggesting I'd be embarrassed or ashamed if I told people about a goal and then didn't do it. Not only is that terribly negative reinforcement, it simply doesn't work.

Think about the last time you enthusiastically told someone about a goal you set. Did they laugh in your face and tell you that you're delusional? Likely not and, if they did, best to remove that person from your life anyway. On the contrary, most people respond in a supportive, almost cheerleader-like manner. When that happens, you get a nice dopamine boost—the same kind you'd get if you hit the goal. For many people, those little dopamine hits from their cheerleaders trick them into the feeling of accomplishment, without the actual accomplishment.

I remember when I started writing my first book. I told everyone about it and received congratulations from everyone. It felt amazing! Privately I thought, "Please say that again when I'm handing you the actual book." Instinctively, I worried if people congratulated me too much, I'd lose interest and move on to something else. So I stopped telling people about it and put in the work one day at a time. The most I would do is post a weekly word count on Instagram because I had a few friends who would see that and offer the right kind of encouragement. Instead of congratulating me on writing a book, they'd encourage me to keep going or tell me they were excited to read it when it was done.

These days, my style is more like Sun Tzu's observation: "Let your plans be dark and impenetrable as night, and when you move, fall like a thunderbolt." In other words, keep your goals to yourself and when you've completed your work, let the results fall onto the world. If you must, tell only a select few what you're up to if you can be certain they will support and encourage you to follow through to the end.

Unfortunately, this means you must leave some of your friends and loved ones in the dark. I've found that those closest to us can unintentionally show up as discouraging when what they are really doing is expressing their own fear and projecting it on to you.

When doing quarterly and yearly forecasts, bigger goals are going to be on the table, and I don't want you to establish them only to quit, or become discouraged, or unconsciously stall out because enough people congratulated you too early.

Now, if you understand the Weekly Forecast process, you already know how to do the quarterly and annual forecasts. It's essentially the same process, but from the point of view of an expanded time frame. As the time frame expands, you'll go deeper into your forecasting, so the quarterly process will take more time than weekly and yearly will take more time than quarterly.

The Quarterly Forecast Process

Think of the quarterly forecast process as a retreat. At a minimum, you'll need a half day uninterrupted to complete the process. And while it's certainly fine to do this on your own, if you have a partner or spouse, I'd recommend bringing them into the process.

I'd also recommend getting out of your day-to-day space and going somewhere where you can't get distracted by your normal routines. If you can swing it, leaving town works really well. That's what we do. My partner, Jon, and I go some place we enjoy visiting for about four or five days. While there, we get up as usual and go through our morning routines; then we sit down and go through the quarterly forecasting process together.

None of our typical distractions are present, so we have space and time to truly focus on the process. Our goal is to make sure that we are on track individually but also that we are in alignment with each other, that our individual actions are likely to add up to the life we say we want to live together. Going that deep requires extended blocks of undistracted time.

At 1:00 p.m. we stop (you knew I was going to say that) and go enjoy the city we're in as if we were on vacation, but we don't go too crazy because, the next morning, we're up at the normal time to build momentum in the day with our morning routine. Then we continue forecasting again until 1:00 p.m. For us, four to five days of that pattern is what's needed to complete an honest forecast for the next quarter.

Here's the quarterly forecast process step by step. You can take this and build an agenda out of it. As you do each of these steps, be open and honest with yourself and then communicate that honesty to your partner or spouse if they are with you. That will trigger deeper understanding of each other and a stronger sense of connection and purpose. By the way, you can use this exact template in a purely professional setting if you're guiding your team. (Visit *donebeforeone.com/bonus* for free template downloads.)

Record Your Wins

Like the Weekly Forecast, you start the quarterly version by recording your wins. Although in this case, you have a chance to expand beyond a seven-day period. Thinking back over the last ninety days, what are you most proud of?

Review Your Performance

Each quarter, you should be roughly a quarter of the way to your goal. Some businesses have bigger fluctuations between the seasons where income is overweighted compared to other times of the year. Either way, this is the time to take stock and look at the numbers. Sometimes people avoid numbers because they know they won't like what they see. But you can't hide from numbers. Even if you don't look at them, they'll still influence your life. So, good or bad, you might as well face them. At the end of the day, they are only a representation of the past, showing you where you can improve.

In addition to sales numbers and profit and loss statements, review your personal goals. If you have a goal of getting back your favorite hobby, openly talk about your experience. Did you play tennis once a week or not? If not, why? For any goal where you're significantly off track, think deeply about whether you still want to accomplish it. If the answer is no, it's far better to drop it than force yourself to pretend for the rest of the year.

Review Your Yearly Goals

Based on your quarterly performance, do you feel your quarterly goals will allow you to hit your yearly target, or do you need to make adjustments? Most people find they are ahead of schedule on some goals and clearly behind on others. If you acknowledge where you stand, you can make good decisions for the next quarter. Often, people refer to this as a gap analysis. As the year wears on, I've found there are times when some things I said I wanted are no longer true. It's not always the easiest thing to do, but if during this review, a goal no longer excites you, now is the time to give yourself permission to drop it altogether.

Establish New Quarterly Goals

So, given what you just learned, what must you do to get back on track in all areas in the next ninety days? That's the only question you need, if you answer it honestly, to determine what must be done in the next quarter. It's exactly how you'll determine your top three for the next quarter.

This is also the time to think forward into the calendar and make sure you're aware of major events and deadlines. Holidays, vacations, contract deadlines, and school schedules all fall into this category. The average person uses such events as excuses why they can't stay on track. If you're living a Done Before One lifestyle, special events don't phase you because you've incorporated them into your life.

Review Your Weekly Time Budget

Once a quarter, it's a great idea to step back and look at your time budget. Is it still working for you?

Look back through your calendar over the last ninety days and notice what's working and what isn't. Does anything need to change? Or do you just want to try something new? The important point is to give yourself the freedom to change and adjust. When something isn't working, switch it up. Each quarter, you have another chance to adjust as your life changes and grows and that interval is frequent enough to make sure you're spending your time on the planet in a way that makes you happy.

Optional: Review Your Journal

Not everyone will want to do this, but I enjoy rereading my morning journal pages once a quarter. I don't pore over every word and I rarely share what I've written, but it gives me a greater sense of self-awareness. I'm able to see how my mindset ebbed and flowed and how that affected my performance. It gives me an idea of where I need to work to grow as an individual. It shows me what I might be resisting or what I might need to let go. It also reminds me of what I'm grateful for because rarely does a morning pass where I don't write out a few lines about gratitude.

The Yearly Forecast Process

The yearly version of forecasting takes the most time and, for me, is the most fun. Most people work on their yearly goals in January, after the fun of New Year's Eve has passed. I learned in real estate that January was way too late. In that industry (and any business with a longer lead cycle) most of the work you do in December shows up on January's books.

November is the true last month of the year. It's the last month you can do anything meaningful to affect the current calendar year. Because of that, we used to have a New Year's Eve celebration on the last business day of November. It was a clever little trick to get us to complete our business plans for the next year in time to line up the production in December.

So if you're in real estate, mortgage, title insurance, legal, or even financial planning—a business that requires longer periods of time to nurture a lead into a revenue-generating customer—consider using November as the end of your year. And if your leads turn over quickly, aim to get your yearly forecast done within the first two weeks of December. That way, you can truly enjoy the holiday season, knowing that you have set up your new year and it is waiting for you to return.

The yearly forecast is going to, of course, look similar to the quarterly process, but it also has some critical tweaks that are important once a year.

Your Dream Life

Once, when talking with my mentor Dr. Wayne Dyer about goals, he told me he no longer set long-term goals. I'd begun telling him about my ten-year master plan that I was so proud of creating when he stopped me and asked where I bought my crystal ball. Huh? Then he asked how I knew who I was going to be and what I'd want a decade from now. I didn't have an answer.

He continued to tell me about the first time he realized he was at a place both professionally and personally that he would never have guessed ten years prior. In fact, he said, remembering what he claimed to want ten years ago made him a little sick to his stomach. He was really glad he hadn't hit those goals because he'd grown and changed and he no longer wanted what he once did. From that point forward, he was no longer willing to set specific goals further out than a couple of years and encouraged me to consider the same.

Turns out, it was the best advice.

So, in this first step, it's time to dream about your future life, without specific timelines. Creating a vision of your dream life is about identifying all the aspects of your life that you would love to be living if you had a magic wand that would make it all come true.

Your dream life list should make you smile when you write it out, and it should freak you out a little. All of us have dreams we know we'd love to live or experience in life, but a part of us deep down harbors some doubt. That's normal. But if you can't even allow yourself to imagine that dream life for a little exercise no one else will see, there's no chance it'll ever happen for real.

Think about all the important categories in life and start writing out the milestones you'd like to manifest. You have your profession, your friendships, your marriage or partnership, your finances, your physical and emotional health, your social life, your hobbies, and your intellectual health.

Review the Past Year

The next step is to review the year you just completed. Whereas writing out your dream life can be a fun and fast exercise, you should slow down and take your time reviewing the past year. Did you have any big wins? Write them out and reflect on what it took to get those wins. Give yourself credit for the progress you made just like you did on a quarterly basis.

Next, compare what you said you would do to what you actually accomplished. Is there a gap? How big? If the gap is huge, were you dreaming to the point of being ridiculous or did you give up?

For example, I'm forty-eight years old and love tennis but have only been playing for a couple of years. I may dream of winning the US Open, but we all can agree that would be ridiculous—even if I refused to give up. But if my goal was to earn a million dollars for the year and I didn't hit it, it would likely be because I gave up. That's not a ridiculous goal for anyone these days.

What if there is no gap or what if you wildly exceed your goal? Take an honest look at whether you pushed yourself enough, or if you have underestimated your true potential. A gap analysis sounds so corporate, but it's one of the best tools you have to build your life as you see fit.

Then, with your wins and your gap analysis fresh on your mind, you're ready to consider the lessons you learned. What did you learn about how you respond to adversity? What seems to motivate you naturally? Did you learn you don't really want all of what you said a year ago? Have you found new projects and activities you'd like in your life? What did you learn about your personal relationships, your physical health, and your mindset? How about your finances? Any lessons to be learned in that category?

Take the time to write out each one so you can see it in black and white.

Annual Goals

Now you're ready to focus on your goals for the next year. Based on what you just achieved and what you learned about yourself and especially your newly described dream life, what do you want this year to look like? You're not the same person and it's not the same year. One of the greatest gifts you can give yourself is permission to grow and change.

For each of the following categories, decide if you want to establish a goal and what it will be.

- Professional
- Marriage or Domestic Partnership
- Family
- Finances
- Physical and Emotional Health
- Friends and Social Life
- Hobbies

This is your yearly forecast, so I'm not suggesting you must have a goal for each category. Work with the categories that inspire you now and add your own if you like.

When setting up your goals, remember that to be effective, the goals must be specific, measurable, attainable, relevant, and time constricted (that is, have a deadline). If you're in sales, saying you want to be the top producer in your company isn't specific enough. What did the top producer produce last year? Are they likely to produce more this year? So what does your gut say you will need to produce to ensure you've got the best chance to be top dog this coming year?

When you have a number, it becomes something you can measure. Now, is that number attainable for you? Meaning, is this your first year in sales? Are you starting from scratch or do you have a solid base and simply need to apply yourself? I'm not saying it's impossible, but listen, if you're a rookie in your industry, you aren't likely to outperform the rock stars in your first year or two. That's what I mean when I say your goals should be attainable.

Relevant simply means important to you. Goal-setting should be so intensely personal that your goals feel selfish. That's hard for many because we attach negative sentiments to the word *selfish*. I do not. I believe selfishness with the proper mindset is necessary. In other words, if I selfishly do what I need to do to take care of myself and live a happy life, I'll then be in a perfect position to help others do the same. It doesn't matter if by others we're talking about family or close friends or strangers even. Until you get your life together, all talk about helping others is nonsense.

Expose Your Doubts

By now, you should be feeling confident about the next year. You've allowed yourself to dream up the ideal life and reviewed your past year, acknowledging what went well and what didn't. You've established fresh goals based on who you are at this moment. Now it's time to expose your doubts.

We all have them. Some people refer to them as limiting beliefs, but whatever you call them, they can impede your progress, so let's shine a light on them. Doubts have a hard time living when they can't hide in the shadows. That's because we all know, on some level, our doubts are just stupid. They aren't even real. They're just fears running out of control, trying to keep us safe from some fictional danger. To expose our doubts, go back through your goals and be real with yourself. What are you afraid of if you give it your all? What excuses are you already lining up just in case you need them? Once they're all out on paper, it's time to play a game.

Pretend your spouse or your child or best friend is expressing these doubts to you. What would you say to them? Whatever it is, I bet it would be encouraging, wouldn't it? Well, can you encourage yourself? One of my mentors says that every subject is really two subjects: the having of something and the absence of it.

When you're in a mental space of doubting yourself and your ability to reach your goals, you're focused on the absence of achievement. That's focusing on the wrong end of the stick. And because it's your mind, you get to choose at each moment which end of the stick you'd like to focus on. For each doubt, what is the opposite? I call those belief statements. They're really just a form of positive affirmation, but in this context, I refer to them as belief statements because they directly refute the doubt carried in your mind.

Translate Annual Goals to Quarterly Goals

Okay, the last step in your annual forecasting process is to take your annual goals and break them into smaller quarterly goals. This isn't always as simple as taking a revenue goal or a sales goal and dividing it by four, although it can be. Before you do that, think through factors like seasonality in your business.

Think about times of the year when you know you're more focused. For example, parents often need to plan around the summer because with the kids out of school, summer production naturally slumps, making it critical to shift more of your annual goals into the first, second, and fourth quarters of the year.

Remember, you have your quarterly forecast to make any adjustments you need along the way, so break up the goals the best you can for now with particular emphasis on the first quarter. For each of your quarterly goals, what are your top three tasks that need to be completed? Sound familiar? I told you we were going to build this process into a loop, didn't I?

One last thing. For each quarterly goal, what reward can you give yourself for hitting that goal? It doesn't have to be huge. For example, my quarterly goal when writing this book was to put in at least one hour per weekday, with no exceptions. When that's done, my reward was to buy a Montblanc leather portfolio I'd been wanting. To me, it felt like an appropriate award for that level of achievement, and it's a reward that has at least something to do with writing.

You can do this for all goals, including personal goals. One of my goals is to learn Italian, and I aim to be fluent enough to confidently move around Italy. As a reward for achieving this goal, I have planned a summer trip next year. It helps if the reward you choose contributes in some way to the life you dreamed up at the beginning of your annual forecast.

Going from Understanding to Knowing

In Part I, I've taken a bottom-up approach to productivity, starting with learning to control just the first half of the day and ending with a comprehensive process to forecast an entire year. But just because you understand something doesn't mean you know it.

To truly know anything, it must be learned in the body, and that only happens by taking action. For example, at one point in your life, the act of driving a car took all of your mind's power, especially if you learned on a standard transmission. But I'm certain today you drove to work without consciously thinking about what you were doing. In fact, you may have even combined driving with the act of eating, putting on makeup, scrolling through social media, or reading something online. I know it's awful and we all do it.

My point is that you used your mind to learn and understand how to drive a car, but you used your body to know it.

But taking action on bigger life goals, especially when you're applying something new, is going to bring up more resistance than a teenager's goal of getting a driver's license. That's what we're going to work on next: overcoming the resistance that's waiting for you right around the corner.

PART II:

SETTING YOUR MIND FOR SUCCESS

8

CONFRONT RESISTANCE AND ADVERSITY HEAD ON

Adversities are life's method of delivering what you've asked for. In other words, when you have a desire, life lines up a problem for you to solve or people for you to help.

Think of this second part of the book in terms of personal coaching. Even if you and I never end up in a coaching session together, I imagine you turning to this section when you need help to implement the Done Before One method.

I was never personally coached by Robert Kiyosaki on financial matters or Seth Godin on marketing or Napoleon Hill on mindset and success principles, but I've returned to their books over and over and used them instead of personal coaching.

In that vein, with me as your virtual coach, we're going to start at a place where people most commonly get stuck. By the end of this chapter, you'll know

- Why you resist change and how to recognize the many forms of resistance,
- How to use the concept of pain versus pleasure to manage resistance, and
- How to use adversity to your advantage.

Why You Resist Change and Improvement

My mentors taught me to recognize resistance in myself early on. Long before social media and the concept of impostor syndrome became prominent in culture, I was forced to confront intense resistance as I learned the art of salesmanship in the residential real estate industry. When I became a performance coach, I got a front-row seat to observe and guide thousands of aspiring, self-employed people down that same path.

You only need to look at the failure rate in real estate to see how tough it is. According to the National Association of REAL-TORS, 75 percent of new agents leave the business within the first year, and by year five, that number goes up to 87 percent. That means out of every 100 agents, only thirteen successfully overcome resistance and get a shot at a long-term career. The resistance those few overcame—that in fact any successful business owner in any industry must overcome—includes fear of failure, rejection, and, most of all, fear of success.

Resistance also shows up as self-doubt, guilt consciousness, comparing yourself to others, worrying about what others think of you, procrastination, and feelings of inferiority and unworthiness.

Resistance is the totality of your conditioned thought patterns trying in vain to keep you safe. When you're first born, there's little to no resistance. Then, as you grew, your parents and society at large worked to condition your thought patterns. In an honest attempt to keep you safe, your parents downloaded their own limiting beliefs.

As you grew up and expanded your circle of relationships beyond the family, society downloaded its limiting beliefs to you in order to keep itself safe. Society does this because if we all buy into our cultural norms and no one ever breaks out taking a risk on something new, then the collective is safe. In both cases, this downloading and programming happens unconsciously.

To be successful as a self-employed individual, you must awaken and learn to identify your unique mix of resistant behaviors. Life itself is expansive and doesn't want to be limited, which is why resistance feels bad, like a nagging, persistent force weighing you down. Think of resistance like the training wheels on a bicycle. For a time, you need them, but once you've advanced to a certain level, the wheels do nothing but hold you back from reaching your true potential. Human beings left the training-wheel stage long ago.

Comparing ourselves to others, being afraid of rejection, standing out too much because of our success—that is, resistance—all stem from a primal need to stay safely in our lane so as not to be cast out of the tribe into the wilderness by ourselves. Without the tribe, we wouldn't survive. Modern society has advanced faster than the primitive part of our brain, which is still doing an excellent job of trying to keep us safe. No wonder we need a little help.

As you learn to become more aware of the specific kinds of resistance showing up in your life, you can make improvements. But beware, there are benefits to resisting change and improvement. The concept of the Done Before One lifestyle is simple to understand, but for most people, it's difficult to implement in their daily lives at first. If I gave you a blueprint without helping you understand how people unconsciously sabotage themselves, your odds of sticking with it long term would plummet.

To start, understand that discussions of others' perfect daily routines are so attractive because they provide an excuse not to commit to something. Resisting commitment by jumping around to every new daily routine you bump into, especially if it's marketed well and comes with a planner, is an easy trap to fall into. I am not oblivious to the irony of the fact that you and I are engaged in that very dynamic. One of my goals is to sell you on adopting a Done Before One lifestyle so that any jumping around you have done before ends.

I have yet to see a perfect daily routine system that addresses the benefits of non-adoption. The reason a person would start using a daily routine enthusiastically, then pretty quickly misinterpret that routine as too restrictive and drop it, is because commitment to the routine itself cuts off some attractive benefits.

For example, every routine I've ever seen includes time to do important work that you'd rather not do. Every profession has "those activities" we resist. Prospecting, preparing for a presentation, having tough conversations, calling customers with complaints, or sitting still long enough to finish administrative work are examples. So the reason people give up so quickly on any routine is because they haven't taken a good look at the temporary, but very real, benefits of self-sabotaging behavior.

Realizing how you're getting in your own way puts you in a position to let go of behaviors that don't serve you anymore. Here are some examples:

- **Engaging in busy work still feels like work**. When you aren't sure what to do or are afraid of what you know you need to do, getting "busy" with nonessential tasks is a clever little trick to make the ego think it's doing something important. Have you ever seen a perfect routine include busy work? I haven't either.

- **Avoiding rejection**. Regardless of your industry, selling your product or service is the number one priority, and sales, of course, exposes you to rejection. Someone may hang up on you when prospecting, unsubscribe from your marketing newsletter, decline to take a meeting with you, reject your effort to sell them your service, or simply ghost you and hire your competitor.

Unless you were born with the thickest of skins or have gone through master-level sales training, rejection is likely something you'll avoid at all costs. Ignoring your block of time for prospecting provides temporary relief.

- **Avoiding failure**. Similar to avoiding rejection, resisting routines keeps you from facing the humiliation of failure. On an intuitive level, I know you understand failure is an event, not a person, but this is something that must be learned on a deep emotional level. When you resist a routine because you're afraid of failure, it simply means you haven't yet internalized failure as an event, separate from yourself. There is too much focus on yourself and not enough on your current and future clients. It's the opposite side of the coin from an overly egotistical person.

   The only difference between the arrogant jerk who is all about himself and the person who continually holds herself back because of fear of failure is in the outward expression of the ego. In both cases, all the focus is on the self instead of where it should be: on the client you're meant to serve. But once you condition yourself to see failure as an event that doesn't define who you are in any way, and is simply a sign that you're trying, you're able to quickly regroup after each failed event and learn valuable lessons.

- **Avoiding personal relationships**. Lack of an effective routine can turn into workdays that never end. I don't know anyone who makes the conscious decision to work all day and all weekend with little time for any other parts of life. But I know plenty of people unconsciously making that choice because they've learned it helps them avoid dealing with an awful marriage, poor health, a lack of loyal friends, boredom, or anything outside work that is uncomfortable. A well-designed routine won't allow for a workaholic lifestyle and thus cuts off this benefit.

- **Avoiding personal trauma.** At its very best, a well-designed routine goes a long way to providing space for the mind to be still and quiet. This terrifies many people. Think about all the noise and distraction around you that do the opposite. From the moment the alarm goes off, we distract our minds with radio, TV, preparing food, eating food, getting dressed, driving to work with more radio, more coffee at the office, meetings, email and social media, lunch, more meetings, kids' events after school, dinner, chores, more email and social media until finally collapsing into bed. Sounds crazy as you read it, but one benefit is an occupied mind that has no space to deal with uncomfortable thoughts and the emotions they surface.

  The more intense the trauma, the more likely it is you'll do anything to keep your mind distracted. This is not a book about overcoming trauma, but if you can recognize that we all have events in our past that disturb us, and that we've all been guilty of distracting our minds to avoid confronting those traumas, then you can be more intentional about using your routine to assist you in releasing and healing trauma.

  Here's a personal example. I used to tell people my greatest fear was being alone. Then my relationship of twenty-three years ended, and I found myself face to face with that so-called greatest fear. It was awful at first and by that I mean on my knees in the shower, in the ugly cry kind of awful. For a period of time, I ditched my routine and got so distracted it felt like I'd moved backward in life. But one day, possibly because of an act of grace, old habits kicked in and I opened my calendar to block out time to get professional help. Then one day I realized I'd become comfortable being alone, often preferring it.

My fear of being alone came from an unhealed past traumatic experience. Once I transformed that specific trauma, I could get intentional about transforming any other trauma that surfaced, thus reclaiming the lifestyle I'd worked so hard to build.

What else can you think of that you're avoiding? Are there additional resistant behaviors you became conscious of as you read through those examples? The more examples you identified with, the more I like you. It means you're being honest with yourself and frankly, makes you pretty normal. So if you're understanding your resistant behaviors and the benefits associated with them, the question becomes, what do you do?

How to Use Pain and Pleasure

The most effective weapon against resistance is taking action. But, as usual, when a human being is involved, it's never that simple. The concept of pain versus pleasure states that humans do what we do, either to move away from pain or toward pleasure. In other words, the action we take is always conditional.

Pain and pleasure exist on a balance scale that tips back and forth. If I allow myself to have a cheat meal on the weekend, I am clearly tilting toward pleasure. In that moment, my desire for the pleasure of chicken and waffles and champagne, my favorite brunch meal, is outweighed by the pain of what the extra calories will do to my physique, which will not be much at first.

But if I frequently eat cheat meals, eventually the balance of the scales will tip. One day I'll look in the mirror and be unhappy at the fat I can pinch around my belly. At that point, the pain of the added fat outweighs the pleasure of chicken and waffles. Once the scales have tipped far enough in the other direction, that's when my behavior changes and I get serious about my diet.

Now think about your behaviors. Each instance of resisting making positive change is like eating more chicken and waffles. It'll be pleasurable only until the scales tip. You know the scales have tipped when your results at work slip. And once that happens, you'll realize the cost of giving in to resistant behaviors is high enough to motivate you into action.

The way to use the concept of pain versus pleasure to your advantage is to pay attention to which way your scale is tilting and work to keep it from going too far in one direction for too long. You can do this by reframing what you think of as painful.

Nearly everyone I know thinks prospecting for clients is a drag and they resist it like they'd resist getting a root canal. Yet I bet you know a few maniacs who somehow freakishly love prospecting. Are they really freaks? I'd argue they're more likely individuals who instinctively, or through coaching, found a more powerful way to think about the act of prospecting.

There are a couple of ways to reframe prospecting. First, you could take the financial approach. To make the math easy, if you need 500 sales to make $1 million in a year and your close rate is 50 percent, then you're going to have to present your product or service to 1,000 people. This means each of the 500 rejections you receive gets you closer to the 500 sales and thus your income goal.

Another option is to take the people approach. If you believe in what you have to sell (and if you don't, just stop immediately), each of the 500 rejections is getting you closer to finding the 500 people you're going to enjoy helping.

Or why not both approaches? The faster you get to 500 rejections, the faster you will have found the 500 people who need your product or service, and the money you are enjoying by hitting your income goal is a representation of those people you've recently helped.

If you're fine with prospecting but find yourself resisting because of the fear of what others will think of you, reframe this perceived pain in order to get into action. Consider that each human is free to have his or her own thoughts. Not only are we free to have our own thoughts, we're having them all the time. Furthermore, you constantly have your own thoughts about other people, don't you?

Okay, so I'm having my thoughts about you and you're having your thoughts about me. My thoughts are none of your business and your thoughts are none of mine, which means what you think of me is none of my business. Get it? That's the reframe. Your thoughts about me are private and none of my business, so my only actual choice is to do what I need to do and disregard what's going on inside your head. There's a book titled, *What You Think of Me Is None of My Business* by Terry Cole-Whittaker that you should read if the opinions of others are a troublesome issue for you to transcend.

Whenever you become conscious of a perceived pain that has tipped the scales too far and is holding you back, the trick to getting into action quickly is to find the reframe that helps you bring the subject back into balance with pleasure. At the end of the day, you're the only one with the power to control how you use your thoughts. The moment you become conscious of the imbalance, you're choosing to wallow in the pain and stay stuck or find the reframe and reclaim your power.

But don't worry. If you're too stubborn and refuse to do anything, life will come along and knock you into action by delivering adversity.

How to Use Adversity

If resistance is a force coming against you, think of adversity as an event. Worrying about being rejected by a prospect is resistance; losing your biggest client would be an example of adversity. Adverse events come and go while you're left to deal with the aftermath, so it's important to gain an understanding of what adversities really are, which, as you'll see, aren't as bad as you think.

Adversity counteracts resistance to change, especially intense resistance. Those moments when we're digging our heels in and refusing to change are when life loves to present us with adversity big enough to force us into action.

Adversities don't appear at random and out of nowhere. They happen because we're asking for more out of life. That could be more money, more influence, more love, better health, and anything else that you want that you don't currently have. The stronger the desire and the bigger the goal, the bigger the adversity will usually be.

Adversities are life's method of delivering what you've asked for. In other words, when you have a desire, life lines up a problem for you to solve or people for you to help. As you tackle those issues, you open a pathway for life to bring you what you wanted. The trick here is to understand that you get to decide what you want, and life gets to decide how you get it.

Want to earn six figures for the first time in your life? Okay, life will bring you an appropriate amount of adversity in an attempt to deliver the income you want. That will probably look like rejection from prospects, failed presentations, and deals that fall through. All of this adversity carries opportunity for growth. If, rather than running away from it, you see it as a challenge from life to improve your skills, you'll eventually see results.

It isn't always possible to draw a straight line between your desire and the adversity life asks you to overcome. For example, a business partner could embezzle money and leave you with nothing, or you could face a challenge involving your spouse or child. Using the same example, it may not seem connected to your desire to earn six figures.

Sometimes you have to trust life and handle the adversity that's in front of you, knowing that, in the end, you'll see the masterful way life lined it all up. For example, a bad business partner could prompt you to start a new business you enjoy more and that quickly surpasses six figures in sales. Or an adversity with your child could inspire an idea for a new product that sells like hotcakes.

You just never know. The sooner you reframe adversity as life's way, mysterious as it can be, of helping you accomplish your goals, the easier achievement will become.

After about ten years of selling homes in Austin, I experienced dissatisfaction with my work. Even though anyone would have described me as successful at that point, something had shifted. For a while I put on my game face and took care of my clients, but when I'd get to the end of the day, I'd feel drained and uninspired, no matter how much money I was making. I didn't like how I felt, but didn't have an immediate solution.

Then my broker asked me to help her set up a training program for new and underperforming agents. She wanted to bring in the same program that did wonders for my career years prior. Knowing I was still in regular contact with that company, she figured I'd be the perfect person to help her get it set up and persuade other agents to get involved. At the time, my attitude was in the toilet and her request came across to me as just another problem, but I agreed to help anyway in case I needed a favor in return someday.

It's not easy getting a bunch of independent contractors to agree to do the same thing at once, but we pulled it off and a group of roughly eighty agents enrolled in the program. It was during the kickoff event that I realized what had happened.

The dissatisfaction I felt with my business came from a shift in my own desires. Instead of working with buyers and sellers, I secretly wanted to coach and train other salespeople. But that was never a secret I could hide from life, which heard my desire to change careers clearly and lined up a challenge. I wasn't wild about spending hours and hours of my free time helping my broker set up a training program that wasn't going to directly affect my bottom line, but had I not handled that problem, I'd never have reconnected with my original trainer and began a discussion on how to learn to become a coach.

Life is an obedient master. If you have a desire, you can trust life is working to bring you a problem perfectly designed to pave the path to what you want. If you handle the problem, you get to move on to other things. If you resist without dropping that desire, life will try harder to get your attention and keep trying until you listen.

Whether you're simply trying to get a better handle on your days to become more productive or going for the biggest goal you can imagine, learning to use adversity to your advantage is a skill worth developing. The next time you experience what you would call an adversity, ask yourself what problem life is asking you to solve?

9

TECHNOLOGY'S BROKEN PROMISE

When I get lost in my phone, who loses?
Is this how I want to be spending my life right now?

Any discussion about productivity in the modern world would be incomplete without addressing technology and, specifically, our addictions to mobile phones. I should tell you upfront, I don't have a novel solution for you. But I do have a perspective to share and, along with it, a conviction that we must help each other use our mobile technology in a way that ensures it serves us rather than let it lead us around by the nose.

I'll never forget the first piece of technology I bought for my business. The telecom company GTE came to our sales meeting and pitched the room of real estate agents on the benefits of digital pagers. I don't remember exactly what they said to convince us, but I know they were persuasive because nearly everyone who didn't have one yet signed up that day. Now, for a few dollars a month, someone could "page" me if they wanted to talk.

I remember the first time I got paged. The simultaneous beep and vibration startled me while I was driving (don't laugh, this was cutting-edge tech), and I felt a rush to get back to the office and call the number. In those days, if someone was in a hurry to speak to you, they'd add "-911" to the end of their number. Then there were the obnoxious people who would page you continuously until you called back.

If you didn't have a pager, you wouldn't know someone was trying to reach you until you got back to the corded phone to check voice mail. If you're old enough to remember those days, you know it was peaceful compared to the way we communicate today. You could go out into the world for hours and not worry about who was trying to reach you. It was exciting to get home and see if you had any messages on your machine, and I suppose it was also a bummer if you didn't.

What, no friends, loser? I'm a fan of the HBO series *Sex and the City* and every time I see Carrie walk into her apartment and hit the play button on her answering machine, I long for those simpler days, if only temporarily.

But in the 1990s, we were told the pager would make our lives simpler and easier by speeding up communication. You could get to a potential client faster and make more money, the technology companies said. And they weren't wrong.

Communication sped up, and it wasn't long before those same companies were back at our sales meeting to persuade us to buy a mobile phone, which no longer needed to be installed in your car. Now, when we got paged, we didn't have to wait until we got to the office. We could use our bulky mobile phones to call the number right away as long as we could get a signal. [On a side note, why is getting a reliable signal the one thing tech companies can't seem to figure out?] In any case, the pitch was the same as with digital pagers: buy this mobile phone and you'll reach clients faster and make more money.

Anyone in sales knows the one-deal technique. It sounds like this: If this new tech product or service helps you get just one extra deal, it'll pay for itself. I've both fallen for that pitch and used it myself many times. And that extra deal to pay for the phone was important because airtime was expensive. Remember when someone called your office from a cell phone? The receptionist would actually announce they were "calling on mobile," which was code for pick up the phone fast because this is costing someone big bucks.

So now we had pagers, and cell phones, and in theory our lives and businesses improved.

If you were skilled and productive in your field, I'd argue they did improve your outcome. After that, for a period of several years, there weren't any major changes. Cell phones underwent improvements in build quality and size, and eventually we phased out pagers due to the addition of basic text messaging to mobile phones. A few years later, the professional world adopted email en masse, the Blackberry, and eventually "always on" internet. That sounds silly today, but I clearly remember how life sped up when we no longer had to dial in on a modem every time we sat down at the computer.

Attack of the Glowy Rectangles

If you're old enough to remember, this might be a fun trip down memory lane, and, if not, it might sound like a cute bit of history, but the point I want you to take away is that each advancement in technology brought with it a faster pace of life, and we were sold on the idea that tech was universally good for us. Then in the summer of 2007 Apple released the first iPhone. Like everyone else, I coveted mine the moment I saw it and held out as long as I could (roughly three months) before buying one.

Except for text entry, I don't remember life speeding up much because of the first iPhone. It was great using the full keyboard and not having to push the number seven four times if I wanted to type the letter S, but mostly I remember how addicting it was to look at the screen. Once the app store launched, our digital lives dramatically sped up again, but this time, it gave us more reasons to keep staring at the screen. Everything from colors to sounds to images to notifications were used to capture our attention.

By the time social media came along, our addictions were complete. To me, there's no difference between the "For You" and explore screens on social than a drug dealer persuading you to try a hit "free, just for you."

Because so much of the app ecosystem was based on the free-plus-advertising model, the war for our attention entered uncharted territory. Advertisers have always been in a war for our attention, but I can flip the page of a magazine, turn away from a billboard, change the radio or TV station, or even delete an email advertisement much easier than I can pry my eyes away from that glowy rectangle.

My dog Chug! was a puppy when the iPhone came out. He didn't know it was called an iPhone, and he didn't know the bigger ones were called iPads, MacBooks, and flatscreen TVs. I'm sure he simply saw his humans staring at these glowy rectangles all day while he wondered how to fight for attention.

Thinking about it from his perspective got me using the term *glowy rectangle*. In any case, it wasn't a fair fight. Too often, he didn't stand a chance of winning my attention without knocking something over or literally jumping into my lap. Chug! was that once-in-a-lifetime dog that connected with my soul, and I'm not proud of making him work so hard. No doubt you've experienced something similar with a pet or can relate to what I'm saying because of your own human children. Never again do I want any human or pet in my life to fight through the backside of a glowy rectangle to get my attention.

I don't want that for you either. Have you seen parents with their kids at the playground recently? If you had to guess, do their children have their full attention or is it divided between them and a glowy rectangle? Ouch. Truth be told, if we don't help each other reclaim our time and attention, we won't be designing our lifestyles at all. Others will design them for us. Now, because our attention is so thoroughly captured, big tech companies can trick us into selling ads for them. We create the content in the form of images, short- and long-form videos, blog posts, and podcasts, then post those images to platforms like Facebook, Instagram, and YouTube "for free." How nice of them, right? They then sell all that content back to us, as we compete against each other to place ads.

In my opinion, it's a morally questionable practice, but there are other problems. Big tech no longer has to convince us they'll make our lives better or faster or that we'll make more money. Not only are we addicted, but we've discovered other, more powerful reasons to sell ourselves on whatever new tech gets rolled out.

From Addiction to Self-Abuse

Our glowy rectangles make it easy for us to hide from anything in life that is even remotely uncomfortable. They are the ultimate resistance enablers. Let's say you need to call a client and deal with a difficult situation, and the thought of how that conversation might go makes you nervous. Rather than handle the emotion and dial the phone, most people grab their phone and distract themselves.

I used to see this every day when I led in-person workshops for salespeople. I worked hard to convince them of the power of one solid, undistracted hour of phone calls to past and prospective clients. It was the toughest sale I ever had to make.

Picture a room of adults in a sales training course who have paid me to show them how to increase their income. We devoted one hour of the workshop to making those calls, and one would think that creating a supportive environment for everyone to work on building a successful habit together would be a positive experience.

But as soon as I'd start the clock, I'd see people grab their phones and start the scroll-scroll-tap-tap-scroll pattern. For a salesperson, prospecting means possible rejection,. It's an uncomfortable thought that is easily relieved by tapping and scrolling. Think for a moment about how many times just today you've tapped and scrolled yourself away from something you'd rather not feel, think about, or do.

One of those more uncomfortable feelings many of us must face is called impostor syndrome. Impostor syndrome existed long before social media, but it was never such a pervasive part of our culture. Unfortunately, when we flee from uncomfortable emotions and distract ourselves by scrolling and tapping social media, we often end up unconsciously comparing ourselves to others. So rather than being comforted by our chosen distraction, we make the problem worse.

If we felt incapable before our distraction, comparing ourselves to others' perfectly edited posts doesn't make us feel any better. Comparing yourself negatively to others, introducing self-doubt, whether spoken or in thought, is the act of using words against yourself. You are literally attacking yourself.

No wonder my students stopped taking action. They were beating the shit out of themselves. Too many people have an addiction to their phones. They are depressed and have stopped taking action in their lives. This is far from the promise big tech made me when I was sitting in that sales meeting getting my first pager. It's also far from the promise made to you whenever you began using technology.

One argument I've heard in favor of big tech is that its algorithms are only responding to your activity, feeding you more of what you show interest in. I don't disagree with that statement, but here's the problem: our brains are hard-wired to be naturally drawn toward the negative, a fact big tech algorithms easily exploit.

Negativity bias—our tendency to focus and dwell on negative stimuli—is how our brains evolved to keep us safe. That's not going to change anytime soon. Unfortunately, we have to go to extreme measures to avoid getting sucked back in. Tactics like turning off all notifications, setting up time limits for apps, or setting the screen to black and white so our eyes don't respond to all the vibrant color are helpful and can be effective, but when you think about it, should it really be this hard to reclaim our own attention?

Broken promises mean broken trust. It serves us to become consciously aware of these broken promises, not so we can make big tech the enemy or play the role of victim, but to reclaim our own power. Instead of trusting technology to make things better, we can learn to trust ourselves. Tactics like turning off notifications can help, and I'm in favor of any tactic that frees our minds from our phones. But it's not like we can follow standard addiction-breaking advice because we don't want to eliminate our phones altogether. Most of us just want to be able to put it down after we've used it and not lose large chunks of time staring at the thing like a zombie.

That's why trying to solve our problem with traditional addiction-breaking frameworks won't work. Can you imagine trying to apply the 12 steps of Alcoholics Anonymous to your mobile phone usage? It just doesn't fit, which is why I believe we all need to answer two foundational questions before we expect any tactics to work long term:

When I get lost in my phone, who loses?

Is this how I want to be spending my life right now?

In my case, I had a breakthrough when I noticed how Chug! was the one losing most often when I was lost in my phone. But he certainly wasn't the only one. Over the years, my friends and family have lost my attention as well. Who in your life has been losing you? If the answer bothers you, you'll be more likely to use tactics to guard against that loss.

Also consider that you could be losing as well. Picture your-self coming out of the store and getting into your car. Do you always buckle up and drive away, or do you ever grab your phone first? How long have you sat tapping and scrolling? Has it ever been long enough that someone wanting your parking spot has honked at you? I can set my phone to prompt me every twenty minutes with a pop-up window asking if it's "Time for a break?" but that's not a powerful enough question. The real question is, "Is this how you want to spend your life?" Unless what you are doing at the moment is intentional, I can't imag-ine your answer would be yes.

Answer both of those questions first, then apply tactics to reinforce your answers.

10

WHY ROUTINES FAILED YOU IN THE PAST
(AND HOW TO MAKE SURE THIS ONE WORKS)

What if you trusted life to do the heavy lifting, and each day you did your best to live in congruence with your inner voice?

I f living a productive and fulfilling life was as simple as following a perfect daily routine, then everyone would hit their goals, thriving and happy. Too much focus on the routine itself leaves out important foundational principles that, when misunderstood, leave you vulnerable to almost any agenda other than your own.

I wish it were as simple as giving you the Done Before One method and calling it a day, but to make any meaningful improvements in your life, you first must understand the most common reasons routines have failed you in the past.

Your Big Why

When was the last time you thought about why you do what you do? To make money, sure, but what do you want to do with that money? The purpose of businesses, jobs, and investments is simply to provide money to live a good life. If you haven't taken the time to define what a good life means to you, you won't know how much money you need to live it. Worse, by default, you'll be working toward someone else's good life.

It's my belief that everyone knows their Big Why. That doesn't mean everyone is honoring it or is even brave enough to state it out loud. What I mean is that everyone knows what they want out of life if they're being honest with themselves. Fear and doubt are powerful forces that keep people's true desires buried deep. If you're not being honest with yourself about the life you really want, what's the point of a perfect daily routine?

I think of a Big Why differently than a person's life purpose. My generation, Generation X, was constantly asked what we wanted to be when we grew up. The energy around that question seemed to be so heavy and serious. It seemed to imply whatever choice we made would be final, and I've struggled with the concept practically my whole life. To this day, I have no answer to what I want to be when I grow up other than I don't really want to grow up. The longer I can channel my inner five-year-old and laugh at fart jokes, the better.

If anything, I'd say my soul came into this body of mine to learn how to drop the need to control everything around me. My life's purpose is to learn to let go and trust my inner guidance, to do what brings me joy, to be of service to others, and, most of all, to pursue a feeling of aliveness.

What would happen if one day at a time, you focused on doing your best to follow the path life wants you to travel? What if you trusted life to do the heavy lifting, and each day you did your best to live in congruence with your inner voice? In that way, you can live out your purpose authentically in the present moment without the need to define it or wrestle it to the ground.

If you like the sound of that, too, then we can drop the whole life purpose bit and allow ourselves to consider what we want right now, in this moment, and why. Another powerful question to consider is this one: What does life want me to do now?

There's a good chance you've heard of the 5 Why's exercise. It's meant to connect you to your authentic desires by asking the same question at progressively deeper levels. You start by stating some kind of goal or expressing a strongly held desire. Let's go through a made-up example to demonstrate:

Stated Goal or Desire: My goal is to earn $1 million per year.

Level 1: Why do you want to earn $1 million a year?
Answer: Because it would be nice to pay off all my debts.

Level 2: Why is it important to pay off all your debts?
Answer: Because my monthly payments make it hard to save money or go on vacation with my family.

Level 3: Why is it important for you to save money and go on vacation with your family?
Answer: Because sometimes I don't sleep well worrying about money. I don't feel safe without a financial cushion, and I'd like my kids to experience other parts of the world.

Level 4: Why is it important for you to sleep well, stop worrying about money, have a financial cushion, and travel with your kids?
Answer: Because when I don't sleep, I tend to be moody, and I don't want to snap at my family. When I have a financial cushion, I feel calmer and happier and able to be present for my family. I want my kids to see how others live so they gain greater appreciation for their own country.

Level 5: Why is all that important to you?
Answer: Because my parents weren't able to achieve meaningful success. I want to break the cycle so we live a good life, and I want to set an example for my children so they can live even better.

Now, looking at level 1 and level 5, which seems more powerful? When you spend as many years studying salesmanship as I have, you learn that people only ever do what they feel like doing. Sometimes we may not want to pay off debt, but when would a parent ever not want to live a good life as an example to their children?

The best thing about the 5 Why's exercise is that you can easily change it as you change. Changing your life purpose sounds daunting compared to allowing goals and desires to evolve and change. In fact, if you believe your life's purpose is to listen to your inner guidance, allowing for change is essential. And as you change and grow, the 5 Why's exercise will help you connect with profound levels of motivation and meaning.

So profound that I've seen many people get blocked after only a couple of levels. What's almost always happening is fear and doubt are triggering limiting beliefs, which stop the exercise in its tracks. The only way I know around this is to go somewhere private where you won't be interrupted and discipline yourself to face the page. When I say face the page, I mean writing down whatever it is you would like to accomplish answering the 5 Why's and then looking at it in black and white.

Forget about how many levels you need when doing this exercise. It may take five or it may take fifty attempts at answering "Why do you want that?" before you've gotten to the core. The important point of this exercise is to decide that you deserve to acknowledge what's in your heart, because no matter how deeply you've buried it, your core desires and your passion are in there. In that private space, you can allow them to surface.

Accountability Is an Inside Job

I can always tell when someone hasn't taken the time to face themselves. They're the people always looking for accountability. When a person isn't clear on why they want what they say they want from life, they approach coaches like me to fill the gap.

If a salesperson wants to earn more commission but doesn't know why they want that, they'll go seeking accountability. They think that someone else will wave a magic wand that will cause them to earn money. If a person wants to lose weight but isn't clear about why, they'll seek a fitness or nutrition coach for accountability. Again, they think the coach is going to cause the weight to come off.

The problem is that coaching can't provide accountability because accountability is an inside job. Pushing accountability off to others is naïve at best and lazy at worst.

Granted, there are hordes of coaching professionals who don't understand this themselves and will take money all day to hold people accountable, but this is about the lowest level of coaching I can think of because it doesn't require any skill—and it doesn't work, anyway. It's basically a lie. So here's the truth. A coach can hold you accountable for a short period while you're learning something brand new, but beyond that, you must generate your own accountability from within.

I have never been approached by a driven person asking me for accountability. Driven people who are clear on what they want from their business, from life, and know their Big Why, use coaching completely differently. They hold themselves accountable because they've gotten clear on their Big Why.

Because of that, in coaching sessions, they bring struggles they're currently experiencing in the field with an intention of working together with their coach until they find the answers.

Or they've identified something new they wish to learn and approach the coach intending to develop a specific skill. But they never ever say to the coach, "I'm having trouble getting motivated and think I need to have someone hold me accountable."

Motivation Is Self-Generated

Motivation is self-generated when you are taking sufficient action toward your goals. If you think about our discussion on resistance, this will make sense to you. Action busts through resistance, and enough action generates motivation. This is why you hear people say that if you wait to take action until you're motivated, you'll never do anything. After eliminating resistance, motivation shows up.

I've worked with many very smart people who have failed to take action and worry if they'll ever find the motivation to build the life they want. Eventually, a lack of motivation can lead to depression, especially if you're addicted to social media and continue to beat yourself up as you watch other people live their best lives (or at least pretend to).

People who have not defined and clarified the life they want to live are not the only ones who suffer from a lack of motivation. Those with a strong sense of purpose and clear goals are sometimes more susceptible to a lack of motivation. The fears and doubts that can keep you from facing your own Big Why can also stop you from taking action once you define it.

That might sound contradictory at first, but I've seen it over and over in coaching sessions with highly ambitious people. If you can somehow overcome your resistance to being honest with yourself about the life you want to live, the next point of resistance typically comes when you start worrying about what others will think of you if you go after it in a big way: Who am I to have that lifestyle? What if no one cares? What if they think I'm too old, too young, too experienced, inexperienced?

Well, let me just tell you, people will think all those thoughts and more. Some may even say it or type it out in comments online. And you have to grow to a point where you can say, "So what? Screw those miserable people who have nothing better to do than obsess over me." Haters hate because they are behind you. No one truly successful will criticize you for going after your goals, so why would you give even an ounce of attention to the haters?

You have to learn to focus on those who need your product or your service because, I promise, they are out there. The world is home to over 8 billion people. Do you really believe what you offer won't help any of them? Your people are out there and you'll find them when they hear your voice. That's only going to happen if you take action. Are you seeing a theme here? Take action to overcome resistance, stay in action to generate motivation, and double down on action when self-doubt creeps in.

Whatever negativity comes back to you because of putting yourself out there isn't about you, anyway. It's about the other person. Learn to stop taking on other people's shit. Lucky for you, there's an easy way to do that. It's called the Focus Wheel.

The Focus Wheel

The most powerful tool you have to build whatever life you desire is your mind. Unfortunately, few people know how to use their mind power, and we certainly aren't taught how as we grow up. Actually, the exact opposite happens. We're born into the world mostly free of baggage (unless you believe our soul carries energy forward) and slowly become conditioned with the limiting beliefs of others. Society and those closest to us are powerful influencers.

Recently, I visited my niece (age eight) and nephew (five). First, I went to my niece's school and sat with her class for lunch. I got a front-row seat to observe the minds and actions of third graders who'd already become highly conditioned. One little girl feared germs on the table and wouldn't touch any food that dropped off her plate. My outburst of the three-second rule was met with a blank stare. Another little girl was already highly concerned about fitting in with others, and the girl next to her was so worried about being treated unfairly that she was counting the pieces of candy each girl got to make sure it was equal.

Across the way was a group of boys, and two of them stood out. One little boy clearly wanted all the attention and would barely let the others talk. The other seemed like he'd pass out if you gave him any attention. In one quick lunch with third graders, I observed fear of germs, fear of not fitting in (criticism), fear of being unacknowledged (the extroverted boy), and fear of being judged (the quiet boy). These fears are learned behaviors, which means that none of these children were born with them.

Now contrast that with the experience I had the next day visiting my nephew, just three years younger, for lunch at his preschool. I'll admit I haven't been around many kids that age and was unprepared for what happened. When I walked into their space, the first thing I noticed was every child going on high alert. Who was this strange adult who just appeared unannounced? It was a primal survival instinct on display.

But once they discovered I was their classmate's uncle, the class deemed me safe and instantly surrounded me. I mean, they were literally hanging onto my legs or in my face asking questions, laughing, telling me random facts about themselves, or telling me how I looked like their dad or brother. The group ganged up on me and literally pulled me down to their level.

Soon after, when we went to their tyke-sized picnic benches for lunch, we all ate spaghetti and the cupcakes I brought. An hour later, I left an exhausted mess needing a shower and a washing machine. By comparison, preschool is one thousand times more fun than the third grade! The preschoolers were full of life and moved about joyously. The third graders weren't having an awful day, but they were already acting reserved and suppressing their personalities.

The people who raise us do the best they can, you have to believe that. You also have to acknowledge that they push, not maliciously, but they push their own limiting beliefs on us to keep us safe. Their heart is in the right place even if their influence is misplaced. At least from my experience that week, it seems like those limiting beliefs take hold somewhere between ages five and eight. Now that you're an adult, it's your job to honor those who raised you and improve yourself from the point they left off.

The ability to take over where your parents left off and move beyond the limiting beliefs you unconsciously adopted requires acknowledging you did, in fact, take on certain beliefs that hold you back. If you constantly heard "money doesn't grow on trees" while growing up, and now believe that money is scarce and difficult to obtain, you must acknowledge your own role in developing that belief. Yes, as a child, you were highly influenced, but you still accepted that influence. You always had the choice about what to think, whether or not you were conscious of it, just as you do now.

Overcoming limiting beliefs also requires a realization that you aren't your mind and that the noise in your head isn't who you really are. You are a part of life, collective consciousness, a child of god, say it however you want, and separately your mind is a tool.

For many of us, it's a tool that's running out of control. Just like my nephew and his class of five-year-olds, if they know they aren't being watched, they'll run out of control. The same thing happens with the human mind. An unexamined mind usually works against you, if only because evolution has caused our mind to prefer focusing on the negative inputs to keep us safe.

I'm going to make an educated guess you've heard a motivational speaker or perhaps a preacher say something like, "Your thoughts control your emotions, emotions control your actions, and actions control your results." That's the Focus Wheel.

But usually, when people discuss the Focus Wheel, they tend to leave out the most important part. How exactly do you maintain consistent control over your thoughts? The answer is to control the inputs you experience throughout the day.

An input is any stimulus you pick up with your five (or even six) senses and then translate into thought. If you hear a news report about a politician that triggers anger, it's the news report that was the input. If you read an inspiring quote that lifts your mood, the quote was the input.

So let's work backward on that Focus Wheel. If you want better results in your life, you're going to have to improve the quality of your actions. The only way you'll do that is to get into an emotional state where you feel like taking improved action. This is important: humans will only do what they feel like doing, then justify their actions with logic to make themselves feel better.

The only way to take control of your emotions is to direct them with your thoughts, and the only way to control your thoughts is to manage the inputs coming through your environment.

This should be hopeful news. I'm saying that if you want an improved result for anything in your life, it's a simple matter of deliberately controlling the inputs. Energy flows where attention goes. Your most direct point of control over your life is where you place your attention—on which inputs you choose to focus. You can trust the sequence of the wheel to take care of everything else. Results aren't always instant—okay, they're rarely instant—but they come.

Go on an Information Diet

Often, controlling your inputs starts with taking a hard look at what you should remove from your life. Think of it as putting yourself on an information diet.

Remember, everything on your phone or on the radio or TV is an input, and those inputs come from another person's mind, not yours. Your family, friends, and coworkers send you inputs when you interact with them. When you read, you are receiving inputs, and when you go out into the world, everything you observe is an input.

An easy way to start your information diet is to pay attention to the way you feel when inputs come your way. When you finish scrolling through social media, do you feel better or worse? When you finish the podcast or news program, how do you feel? When you read that blog or that book, are you inspired or not? When you interact with that person, are you energized or drained?

Negative emotion is the way life is telling you the input is not good for you. It's life's way of showing you where you may need to make some edits. Weeding out the inputs that aren't making you feel good creates space for new inputs to come into your life.

Odds are you don't need those mainstream news emails or the shopping messages that constantly sap time and play on your fear of loss by using countdown times to the end of the sale that will just start again the next week, anyway. If you haven't done this in a while, schedule some time to go through your inbox and unsubscribe from all of those emails you know you don't need.

Apply this to your social media accounts too. I want you to be ruthless. If you are following someone and their posts make you feel anything other than hopeful and inspired, unfollow them. Eventually, you'll want to grow to a point where you can see other points of view that you may not agree with and not let them trigger you. Eventually, you should be able to celebrate the success of others without it chipping away at your own sense of self-worth because of impostor syndrome. But for now, it's likely a better idea to unsubscribe and unfollow.

Now, what about podcasts and television? Do you listen to the "news," which we all know is propaganda? If so, you gotta stop that. Unsubscribe from podcasts and turn away from the TV stations that only leave you frustrated at the end.

What about talk radio? This was a big one for me. In the last few years, I swung wildly from what I thought was a fairly liberal political belief system to a highly conservative one, only to learn that it's just two sides of the same coin. The term *"uniparty"* sounds more accurate every day.

I found radio shows on both sides were experts in manipulating my emotions by feeding me inputs that generated unhelpful thoughts. I would consider myself libertarian if a label must be used, but in any case, the past few years have reminded me of the importance of deliberately choosing the inputs you accept into your mind.

Even some of your personal relationships could need to be altered. If a person's energy drags you down every time you interact with them, to the extent you can, cut off or limit your interactions.

There is much for you to control, but sometimes life forces inputs upon you. For example, a person cuts you off on the highway or slows down at a yellow light instead of speeding up (who are these people?). You could be walking somewhere in public and see or hear something disturbing you didn't expect. When this happens, the trick is to learn to replace the negative input with a positive one as soon as you can.

Just like a nutritional diet can help get your body back on track, an information diet can do the same for your mind. The concept is simple: just as you would avoid the foods that make you gain weight, on an information diet you avoid the information (the inputs) that make your mind too heavy.

Some people have deeply rooted patterns, so this may not be easy at first. The more easily triggered you are, the more important this becomes. You can control the environment in your home and office to perfection, but the moment you step out into the world, you lose much of that control. But you will never lose control of your own response to an input. Softening your response to inputs that trigger you negatively takes commitment to putting yourself, your mood, your mental health, your productivity, and your happiness first.

When I started to practice this technique myself, like any good Capricorn, I easily controlled my home and office environments. I cleaned up my email inbox and reduced the number of people I follow on social media to only a few hundred. I ended unpleasant professional relationships, stopped doing work for clients I didn't particularly like, cut out mainstream news, and tuned out of talk radio and podcasts that would aggravate me.

But I still found myself getting disturbed by events outside my control. Like traffic, the behavior of others, and even the weather. It's embarrassing to admit, but there was a time when I would get highly disturbed if the weather wasn't exactly the way I wanted it. Ultimately, I learned my need to control precisely everything was an attempt to feel safe.

I grew up accepting a limiting belief that the world isn't safe, and it manifested for me as feeling I needed control over everything. I worked hard when I was younger, made money, and did everything I could to control the people and situations around me. Looking back, getting into sales was almost inevitable. I couldn't force anyone to do what they didn't want to do, but I became highly persuasive, and that gave me the illusion of control.

Someone suggested that I find a physical symbol to break out of this cycle and free myself from that limiting belief, so I chose the memento mori skull. The Latin phrase *memento mori* translates into "remember death" or "remember that you [have to] die." The first skull I bought was on a beaded bracelet, and the skull quickly proliferated around me. But I have to be honest with you. It hasn't been until recently that this has sunk in to where transformation has occurred. I would consider myself a willing yet stubborn student. It's a good thing then that life is so thoroughly persistent.

Starting in 2015, I experienced a series of actual deaths. First my dad died, then my twenty-three-year relationship ended a painful death, then my professional identity (to which I assigned far too much value) died. Not long after that my mom died and most recently I lost my dog Chug!.

My point is not to generate sympathy here. Millions of people around the world suffer more than I have, but I have become highly aware that each day could be the last. When my mom died, it struck me that if I died the same age as she, I'd only have twenty-three years left! Talk about a wake-up call.

I only tell you that to describe how we all face our own battles so that it can soften us and open us up more fully to life. These days I'm far less likely to resist what I can't control.

The skulls, which I still have around me, instantly refocus my mind toward inputs that make me feel, at the very least, a sense of relief.

Life doesn't have to be so hard. Images or events that we allow to disturb us don't have any power other than what we give them. The Done Before One lifestyle is one where you use your work in the world to provide the funds to live a great life, and living a great life is impossible without awareness that you have direct control over most inputs and the power to control your reaction to the rest.

11

SETTING YOURSELF UP FOR SUCCESS

There is tremendous power in letting go of the past and allowing yourself to act like this is your first day on the job.

Where to Start

We started our time together talking about one single day. No matter what time of year you've come across this book, the first order of business is to get familiar with the Done Before One daily philosophy and practice putting it into place in your life. In my experience, it takes people at least three months to observe enough positive changes to sell themselves on how powerful and life-changing this process can be.

Of course, three months will lead you straight into the quarterly forecast process, and by the time you reach the end of the calendar year, you should have the preparation and readiness to tackle your first comprehensive annual forecast. If you are reading this at the end of the year, there's certainly no problem working in reverse and starting with the annual forecast. That's how most people work through this kind of material, anyway. Just be aware that the power in the Done Before One lifestyle comes from the bottom up. That means your annual forecast gets its power from the quarterly forecast, which derives its power from the Weekly Forecast, which is only possible focusing primarily on getting your most important work Done Before One on a day-to-day basis.

Along the way, use the chapters in Part II to guide you through your natural resistance to change. Except in rare cases, no one actually hits their yearly goals all at once, anyway. If you want to make a million dollars, you'll do it by accomplishing small tasks often enough to add up to your million dollars. So stay focused on the small tasks that you can do now that will lead to big results.

If All Else Fails, Declare a Day One

Sometimes, no matter how charged your phone is, it'll work better if you restart it. When my apps aren't working as they should, restarting the phone usually brings them back to normal operation. Depending on what's going on in your world when reading this, you may need a restart before heading into your new Done Before One life.

You can restart yourself by declaring a Day One. This has become my favorite life hack because it acts as a reset button for those times when you are so frustrated, stressed, or lost you wish you could just start over. Well, guess what? You can start over! Any time and as many times as you want.

The concept of declaring a Day One came from my early days as a real estate agent. After many months of struggling, I'd finally put my first deal together, only to have it fall apart a few days later when the results of the inspection came back and spooked the buyer. I was distraught and my broker tried to cheer me up by reminding me that no matter what happened, I could always go find another deal.

I wasn't exactly buying it, so she encouraged me to quickly get back on the phone and start talking to people. It felt like starting over and I didn't like it one bit. But I found another client, and I eventually learned what every commissioned salesperson and small-business owner learns: every time a deal closes, you're starting over.

So when business wasn't going the way I wanted it to, what would stop me from starting over? The answer was nothing, and I used that mental trick many times over the years. There is tremendous power in letting go of the past and allowing yourself to act like this is your first day on the job. After all, on the first day you're full of optimism and, importantly, haven't had time to mess anything up! So since you're self-employed, just fire yourself and rehire—yourself.

Later, when introducing the idea to others, I found the phrase "declaring a Day One" was easier to understand intuitively. Declaring a Day One creates the mental space needed to get yourself back on track. It's a way of reclaiming your power and getting into action. If you've slipped into a victim mindset, starting over helps you drop that anchor. You are responsible for your life, and when it falls off track, no one is coming to save you.

But that's okay because it means you can save yourself. Declaring a Day One is how you reset mentally so you can start fresh. Mostly when you make this declaration, it's a private moment with yourself—and your journal—but there is absolutely no harm in declaring it to the world, however you see fit.

So whether you need to declare a Day One today or not, here's to a totally new way of life—a Done Before One life. Bottoms up!

Online resources for the major concepts presented
in this book can be downloaded at

www.DoneBeforeOne.com/bonus

ACKNOWLEDGMENTS

This book covers a topic I've wanted to write about for years but always thought people would find too boring or already sufficiently examined in other books. After putting up a pretty good fight, life finally won out by bringing me enough interactions with people to convince me otherwise. I've learned that when it comes to the importance of how we spend our time on the planet—that is, how we spend our lives—there will always be room to write more.

Special thanks to my team of beta readers for spending time reading early versions of the manuscript, helping me weed out confusing spots and identify the most useful sections.

Mallory Mundy, JJ Kennemer, Rose Hayden, Isabel Affinito, Mary Ann Burke, Jamie Matusek, Kristin Thumlert, Benjamin Carolan, Shaunna Terry, Amanda Cowan Sanchez, Isaac Gonzalez, Juan Pablo Hsu, Sasha Hsu, and Joe Harrison.

Thank you, Chris Heagerty, one of my earliest mentors, for accepting me into an environment where, before I was old enough to drink (legally), a group of fifty of the highest producing salespeople in Austin surrounded me. I learned more during those years about how to succeed in business than I ever would have in college.

Thank you to Floyd Wickman and Dr. Wayne Dyer for teaching me about sales, leadership, mindset, and about people. Your lessons have become an integral part of my work today.

Thank you to my partner, Jon, for always believing in me more than I believe in myself and to my angel army who sent ideas and inspiration whenever I asked.

ABOUT THE AUTHOR

J asen Edwards left college after two semesters and at eighteen began working for himself as a residential real estate agent. Surrounded by competitors, he had no choice but to figure out what it would take to succeed as a self-employed individual in a cutthroat industry.

During the first eighteen months, he only made one sale and $6,000 in commission. Then, out of desperation, he enrolled in a three-month sales training program where he learned the art of salesmanship. He outproduced his entire office of seventy-five experienced agents during that training program and earned ten times what he had since first being licensed.

Before he turned thirty, Jasen spent over a decade selling homes in Austin, Texas, achieved the distinction of being the youngest person ever listed on the *Austin Business Journal's* Top 50 agents list, and graced the cover of *REALTOR* magazine. He became the go-to guy in his company for agents needing help and began informally coaching people on how to master sales, control their time, and thrive in other areas of their lives.

Eventually, Jasen realized coaching was more fulfilling than selling houses and became a performance coach and motivational speaker. He mentored under industry legend and Hall of Fame speaker, Floyd Wickman, earning the rank of Master Trainer. In addition to coaching thousands of salespeople, he inspired and helped launch a nationwide training program for the country's biggest real estate company.

Along the way, Jasen spent several years being mentored by self-help guru and "father of inspiration," Dr. Wayne Dyer, who encouraged him to write and expand his message beyond the residential real estate industry. Jasen came to understand, with Dr. Dyer's help, that his coaching work may have started with real estate salespeople, but the message was meant for a wider audience of entrepreneurs.

Now Jasen spends his working hours teaching self-employed people and small-business owners how to gain lasting control over their time, their activities, and their income.

His clients do what most think is impossible: they charge above-average fees for their work, enjoy regular time off, and experience the freedom they dreamed of when they first got into business for themselves.

In 2021, he released his first book, *The Top Producer Life: Build the Real Estate Career of Your Dreams in Any Economy*.

Jasen lives his own *Done Before One* lifestyle in Scottsdale, Arizona, with his partner, Jon, and their dog Hugo.

www.ingramcontent.com/pod-product-compliance
Lightning Source LLC
Chambersburg PA
CBHW071212210326
41597CB00016B/1783